OUR CHIEF OF DAYS

The principle, purpose, and practice of the Lord's day

JEREMY WALKER

Published by EP Books (Evangelical Press)
Unit C, Tomlinson Road, Leyland, PR25 2DY

epbooks@10ofthose.com

www.epbooks.org

© Jeremy Walker 2019

Print ISBN 978-1-78397-246-3

eBook ISBN 978-1-78397-265-4

Scripture taken from the NEW KING JAMES VERSION®. Copyright© 1982 by Thomas Nelson, Inc. Used by permission. All rights reserved.

CONTENTS

Introduction	v
1. The principle of the Lord's day	1
2. The purpose of the Lord's day	41
3. The practice of the Lord's day	61
Conclusion	107
Notes	113

INTRODUCTION

Not long ago, many Christians talked about 'keeping Sunday special.' Today's society—not to mention today's church—seems increasingly convinced that such a concern is irrelevant. In many places people stay away from churches generally. Congregations dwindle. The vast majority of both converted and unconverted men and women appear to approach Sundays with a take-it-or-leave-it attitude. We might ask ourselves, "Why bother with Sundays?" Are there not other, perhaps better, ways of spending our time and expending our energies in the service of God? Why not abandon Sunday worship and go where and when we will find the people? Why not arrange our churches in a way that conforms to and perhaps appeals to the patterns of activity and behaviour we see in our culture and society?

Where can we even begin to find answers to such questions? How do we approach such a topic when there are so many perspectives and opinions in existence? The issue calls forth such different views and approaches. Do we simply rehearse the various positions that one can take, and then leave each Christian to adopt the one which best suits their lifestyle and expectations? Do we choose whichever one is closest to the tradition in which we were raised? Perhaps we should just take the nearest match to the church in which we were converted, or where we are presently in membership? Do we, perhaps, consider all the positions and then try to find some middle ground between them all, on which everyone can agree? Or, do we at least agree to disagree, and then try not to disagree too much?

This short book is written out of the conviction that we do not need to trouble ourselves with such intellectual or ecclesiastical gymnastics to find the answer. We need simply to search the all-sufficient word of the living God. We must do so in dependence on the Spirit of God for the illumination of his book and the enlightening of our hearts. We might fail to realise just how broad is the sufficiency of Scripture. The word of God has a breadth and beauty that meets the deepest, greatest, and most complex needs of mankind. It addresses the issues of faith and life in a manner that is eminently practical. The psalmist knew how to order his life: "I thought about my ways, and turned my feet to your testimonies" (Psalm 119.59).

Are you faced with questions or dilemmas about the Lord's day? Are you concerned about its relevance and value? Do you want to know what to do with it and on that day if it is, indeed, relevant and valuable? Then you need to think over your ways, and turn your feet back to the testimonies of God. The Bible has the answer—not just *an* answer but *the* answer—to such questions. Admittedly, we might not like the answer, but that is not the point. We should not come to Scripture to uphold or to attack any particular conviction or tradition. We do not use the Bible as a kind of (un)holy pick'n'mix display out of which we simply choose the goodies which most appeal to our established taste. We come to it to learn. We come to submit ourselves wholeheartedly, cheerfully, and willingly to what God has revealed of himself. We come to embrace what God has revealed to and for his people, in every aspect of our relationship to him and to each other.

We need to make Scripture the touchstone of our Christian living. We must be reflecting, acting, and going in accordance with God's holy word. This often tempts us to despair when we see the high demands of Scripture. Perhaps we think, "I cannot do that! It is beyond me!" But that is to forget the sufficiency of grace. Consider Romans 6.17-18: a Christian is a slave to righteousness, liberated by grace to what we can call 'evangelical obedience'. What does this mean? Simply that the law is no longer an outward taskmaster but an inward teacher, a true joy, being written on the heart of the Christian (Hebrews 10.15-16). As a result, we now obey from the heart that form of doctrine (observe, not that flood of feelings or collection of vague wishes) to which we have been delivered (Romans 6.17). Obedience is a product of redemption. Unredeemed, we are unable to obey. Saved by grace, a new impulse governs and guides the new creation in Christ, as the old things pass away, and all things are made new.

It is grace we need, and grace we have, in order that we might serve God entirely. Resting on God's grace in Christ, we must not be conformed to this world – its patterns of thought, desire, and behaviour. Instead, we need to be transformed by the renewing of our minds (Romans 12.1-2). Our aim should not be, first and foremost, to become part of a certain tradition, denomination, or group. Our aim should not be to find the balance of all the various perspectives on a particular issue. We are not trying simply to rehearse the view we have always held, or that others have held before us, though we should certainly consider the wisdom of the ages. We should all desire and pursue the binding of our consciences to the word of God alone.

It is this approach that we need to take to the issue of what is often known as 'the Lord's day'. We shall attempt to do so by studying the *principle* of the Lord's day, the *purpose* of the Lord's day, and the *practice* of the Lord's day.

A Particular Baptist pastor called John Sutcliff was part of the revitalisation of Baptist life in the eighteenth century. He was intimately involved in William Carey's development as a preacher and sending as a missionary.

When he wrote to his fellow believers about the Lord's day, he could write with this assurance: "You love that sacred day; it is dear to your very souls."[1] I hope that, in considering this topic, you will come to that same point, to the refreshing and rejoicing of your own soul.

I

THE PRINCIPLE OF THE LORD'S DAY

Where do we get the idea of the Lord's day, or even the idea of a Sabbath day at all? Is the idea of a Sabbath day an Old Testament idea, bound up with the Old Testament laws and no longer applicable today? Are we not under grace, rather than law? Is this not one of the things that has passed away?

If we consider the biblical data, a very different picture emerges from the one that is often assumed.

ESTABLISHED AT CREATION

The idea of one day in seven being set apart ('sanctified') by and for God predates the giving of the Law at Mount Sinai. The Sabbath is one of three so-called 'creation ordinances'. The meaning of this is simple. While still in the created state of innocence, a condition of perfect and sinless communion with the holy God, three great matters were ordained by God and so established for man. One was marriage (Genesis 2:20-25). A second was work or labour (Genesis 2:15). The third (and one which realises a degree of its significance in the context of the ordinance of labour) is that of a sabbath--a rest. There is a close link between the ordinance of work and the ordinance of the Sabbath: God's sovereignty is established over both our strength and our time. This link is reaffirmed in the fourth commandment.

The day God made

We read in Genesis 2:1-3 that "the heavens and the earth, and all the host of them, were finished. And on the seventh day God ended his work which he had done, and he rested on the seventh day from all his work which he had done. Then God blessed the seventh day and sanctified it,[1] because in it he rested from all his work which God had created and made." The idea of rest is not one of weariness or inactivity, but of God ceasing from the particular work of creation.

From the beginning, then, God established by divine act a rest of one day in seven. He patterned that rest in himself. He did not establish it for men as under law, or under grace, as it were, but for men as men. In the words of Robert Louis Dabney, "the professed Christian has two reasons for observing the Sabbath: every human being has one."[2] This is the foundation of all our understanding of and dealing with the Lord's day.

It is worth noting that the first Sabbath was the first

full day of Adam and Eve's existence. "Behold the dignity of the Sabbath!" exclaims Sutcliff:

> How honourable in its origin! Let us look back to the garden of Eden. There we find this sacred day. Take a view of our first parents in a state of innocency. They began their lives, by keeping it holy to God. They gave the first fruits of their time, to their creator.[3]

Their first day of life was spent on a day that God blessed and sanctified, in which he rested from his creative work. They spent their first full day on earth focused on the Lord God.

Bread from heaven

Consider also a passage such as Exodus 16:22-30, about the gathering of the manna, that special bread from heaven which the Lord provided to sustain the Israelites in the wilderness:

> And so it was, on the sixth day, that they gathered twice as much bread, two omers[4] for each one. And all the rulers of the congregation came and told Moses. Then he said to them, "This is what the Lord has said: 'Tomorrow is a Sabbath rest, a holy Sabbath to the Lord. Bake what you will bake today, and boil what you will boil; and lay up for yourselves all that remains, to be kept until morning.'" So they laid it up till morning,

as Moses commanded; and it did not stink, nor were there any worms in it. Then Moses said, "Eat that today, for today is a Sabbath to the Lord; today you will not find it in the field. Six days you shall gather it, but on the seventh day, the Sabbath, there will be none." Now it happened that some of the people went out on the seventh day to gather, but they found none. And the Lord said to Moses, "How long do you refuse to keep My commandments and My laws? See! For the Lord has given you the Sabbath; therefore He gives you on the sixth day bread for two days. Let every man remain in his place; let no man go out of his place on the seventh day." So the people rested on the seventh day.

All this was the case long before the Ten Commandments were given at Sinai. God expected the people to observe the Sabbath, and it was observed, before he gave the Law. Manna was provided, and was to be gathered, on six days. Any manna that was kept overnight on those days bred worms and stank, being intended for that day alone. However, the manna collected on the sixth day remained good, and was able to be eaten on the seventh day. As the people struggle to come to terms with the commandments and laws of God (v28) as a free people, a succession of increasingly explicit revelations is given. God is making provision for the Sabbath to be kept: "the Lord has given you the Sabbath" (v29). In Egypt's slavery there could be no rest, but the redeemed nation is expected to observe that which God ordained, from creation, for all men. Observe also here that once more the Sabbath works out in both Creator and creature. Man's activity is patterned in God. As at the first man rested as God rested, so here God refrains from his customary labour of manna-provision, and the people rest from their customary labour of manna-collection.

The right foundations

If we come to this whole issue as Bible-believing Christians, it is very easy to overlook one vital fact: we have assumed that creation is true. The sabbath ordinance is founded upon a conviction of the literal truth of the creation account. For that we neither need nor should make any excuse. It is literal truth, it is recorded history, and is to be believed as literal truth and recorded history. We see almost in passing the dangerous effect of evolutionary teaching, and other denials or 'reworkings' of the biblical record, in both the world and the church. A denial of the biblical doctrine of creation often (though not necessarily) goes hand-in-hand with resistance to the idea of one day in seven set apart for God. The connection between the two is obvious: if there was no seven day creation, there need be no pattern of resting every seven days. To do away with the Genesis record deprives us of a foundational appreciation of and provision for our humanity. It strips us of the essence of our created humanity as labouring, resting, and enjoying the most intimate of relationships with another, in all of which God himself is our pattern. The creation account is something to which we must cling because it is biblical truth, yes, but also because to abandon that is to abandon our very humanity.

AFFIRMED IN THE LAW

There are three elements of the law given by Moses: a ceremonial aspect, a judicial aspect, and a moral aspect. All of these have been fulfilled in Christ (Matthew 5:17).

The ceremonial law had to do with the ceremonies of the Old Testament, primarily the work of the temple and its sacrifices. The ceremonial law is fulfilled in the finished sacrificial and perpetual priestly labour of the Lord Jesus.

The judicial law had to do with the laws God gave for Israel to conduct itself as a righteous nation under his authority. That now transcends the land geographically and the people nationally. It is fulfilled as principles of general equity and righteousness grounded in the character of God and the conduct of his people (see, for example, Paul's use of the principle that "You shall not muzzle an ox while it treads out the grain" from Deuteronomy 25:4, applying it in 1 Corinthians 9:9 and 1 Timothy 5:18 to the idea of a fair wage for a hard worker).

The third part, the so-called moral law, still preserved in the Ten Commandments, is also fulfilled. The moral law was the word which the Israelites heard in a distinct way on Mount Sinai. This abiding revelation of the holiness of God remains a perpetual rule for the people of God. However, one of the new covenant blessings promised in the Old Testament and realised under Christ is that this law will be written on the hearts of God's people (Jeremiah 31:33 *cf* Hebrews 10:16). Our Lord expounds and applies true obedience to that law, and its proper observance, in Matthew 5-7 (*cf* Romans 7:12).

Freed to obey

There are ten commandments, and obedience to them is established and founded upon Israel's redemption from Egypt. Israel is freed to obey. The ten commandments include one about working for six days and keeping a sabbath rest every seventh day, based on the creation principle of one day in seven (Exodus 20:8-11). Can we act as if, or pretend that there are, only nine commandments? Which Christian would permit or promote blasphemy, idolatry, covetousness, murder, or adultery? On what basis can we then seek to persuade ourselves that we can ignore the fourth commandment? There may be a question as to *how* we keep it, but there can be no question as to *whether* we keep it. This perpetual rule of holiness (now written on the hearts of the new covenant people of God) reminded Israel that – having been freed from Egypt – the nation was to observe the creation ordinance of one day in seven, set apart to God. In the Mosaic economy, that one day was the seventh.

It is important to take into account that we must embrace the whole commandment. It has a positive aspect. We are certainly to "remember the Sabbath day, to keep it holy." However, we are also reminded, that on "six days you shall labor and do all your work" (Exodus 20:9). God has ownership of our time and energy. Pharaoh had kept the nation enslaved, working without cease. But they are God's people: they work at his word, and they rest by his blessing. Too often the positive aspect of the fourth commandment is neglected, but both aspects carry weight. The balance of our time is allotted by the divine command of our Creator and our Redeemer.

We should therefore note that, even here, God's purposes for the day of rest are not linked to creation alone. Moses, reviewing the ten commandments in Deuteronomy 5, gives us additional detail in verses 14 and 15. The Sabbath command has redemptive and covenantal significance in addition to its creative purpose. Israel is to remember that she was a slave in the land of Egypt. The nation should consider that the Lord their God brought them out from the land of their captivity by a mighty hand and an outstretched arm. It is on this basis, as well as that of creation, that the Lord requires the observance of a sabbath: "therefore the Lord your God commanded you to keep the Sabbath day." Redemptive grace operates throughout history in God's dealings with sinful men. Grace liberates and obliges. It redeems man from the slavery of sin, and liberates him for and obliges him to obedience to righteousness (Romans 6:17-18), which becomes both duty and delight. The Sabbath was never a harsh legal imposition—man was not made for the Sabbath, but the Sabbath for man (Mark 2:27). Man was made to enjoy it as a created being, and the capacity and opportunity to enjoy it were restored to him by God's redeeming power.

PERPETUATED UNDER THE LORD JESUS CHRIST

There are several truths which people imagine or hope the Lord Jesus Christ never really addressed. In many cases, he did so repeatedly. One is the doctrine of the Day of Judgement, with an eternal heaven or hell to follow. Another of the topics with which our Lord dealt repeatedly is the Sabbath. We should begin by reminding ourselves that the Lord Jesus observed the Sabbath conscientiously as a Jew. It was his custom to go "into the synagogue on the Sabbath day" (Luke 4:16). In his teaching (Matthew 12:1-12; Mark 2:28) our Lord never once undermined the institution.

In his day, the Lord had to deal with a group of Jews called the Pharisees. These were highly religious Jewish nationalists. The Pharisees typically saw obedience as a way of winning God's favour. The thinking was, "If I do what he says, he is obliged to favour me." They were in the habit of creating rules and regulations by means of which to explain and expand upon what they thought were God's expectations of his people. They did this with the Sabbath of the seventh day. When the Lord dealt with the Sabbath, he stripped off the legalistic and ungodly additions and accretions[5] of Pharisaism in order to restore the day to its original purpose. Jesus did not really argue with the Pharisees about the purpose of the Sabbath. That was, up to a point, common ground, though our Lord clarified and purified it. For the most part, the Lord contended for what that purpose really involved and how it was worked out. In fact, Jesus as Messiah claimed the Sabbath for his own (Mark 2:28).

It is worth noting what our Lord meant when he said "the Son of Man is also Lord of the Sabbath." Is he claiming the right of abolition? Is he saying that, as Messiah, his disciples are no longer obliged to observe it? We noted earlier that the fact that "the Sabbath was made for man" is a positive declaration. So here, our Lord's statement is positive. It is a declaration of confirmation rather than abolition. Observe what Christ has just done (using either of the parallel narratives). He has not attacked the Pharisees for observing the Sabbath. Rather he has exposed them as doing what they so often did: obscuring the true meaning of the law of God underneath a vain heap of human traditions and accretions. What Christ does is sweep away the dross with which the Jews had obscured the original purpose and design of God's creative ordinance. It was restored to Israel by way of redemption at Sinai but since then had been twisted by wrong human interpretations and impositions.

Babylonian thinking

A writer called Bruce Ray has some interesting observations on the Pharisees' abuse of the Sabbath.[6] When the Hebrews were taken into captivity the land of Israel enjoyed the rest that it should have had. It made up the sabbaths, the rest days, that the nation had denied the land by their ungodliness. But a new trouble was developing. Captivity among the Assyrians and Babylonians (especially the latter) perverted Judaism in some respects. The Jews bought back some of those perversions with them. For example, the Babylonians had a twisted observance of certain seven day cycles in certain months (perhaps itself a distortion of God's original Sabbath ordinance). On these days they avoided certain activities in particular, and work in general, because of fear of demons. This Babylonian *shappatu* was a day of fear and gloom, not of joyful celebration. Ray suggests that many of the Jews, in this respect, were conformed to the world (Romans 12.1-2) and began to think like the nations to which they were exposed. After the return, the Jews began to observe the Law not as an expression of redemption, but as a means to redemption. This led to a 'filling out' of the Law, which the rabbis and elders considered necessary in order to explain what God's law meant. Many of these additions to the Word of God are recorded in the Talmud, a record of Jewish oral traditions. The Sabbath tractate, the portion that deals with these days of rest, lists thirty-nine categories of prohibited work, each having thirty-nine separate subdivisions. That makes a grand total of 1521 Sabbath prohibitions! Ray contends that this Sabbath appeared biblical, but was, in fact, substantially Babylonian. It had ceased to be a joyful festival of worship, based on liberation, and became a gloomy day, based on fear and oppression.

In place of these Pharisaic additions and accretions, Christ declares the Sabbath once more in its virgin purity. The Lord Jesus restored the day to its proper meaning and use. He declares that the Sabbath is his day. It belongs to the Son of Man, a title that belongs to him as Lord of all, and not just a Jewish deliverer. It is his as Almighty God, to restore first to his people (and then, by extension, to others) for its original purposes.

Incidentally, here we also see the root of the authority of the Lord Jesus Christ to alter the day of observance from the seventh day to the first, while maintaining its substance and purpose. In Sutcliff's words, "No authority can, with any propriety, be acknowledged, in fixing or appointing the precise time, but that of Jehovah."[7]

As the Son of Man and the Lord of the Sabbath, our Lord cuts through to the original intention and pattern of the day. He sweeps away the sinful additions and obscurities of the years, revealing and giving it once more as it ought to be: a day of blessing, benefit, and comfort.

Fulfilling the law

In similar fashion, we might note what the Lord said during the Sermon on the Mount. He made it very clear that we should not think that he came to destroy the Law or the Prophets. Rather, says our Lord, "I did not come to destroy but to fulfil" (Matthew 5:17). He was not saying there that the law had been fulfilled by him and that we need no longer concern ourselves with it. In effect, that would be to interpret the passage as saying, "I did not come to destroy but to destroy."

Christ's basic point is that what he does, teaches, requires, and accomplishes is in harmony with the Old Testament. It appeared to the law-obsessed scribes and Pharisees that the Lord was, in his teaching, doing away with the Law as they understood it. Our Lord responds to their criticism before they have made it. He has not come to destroy the Law—all or any of it, ceremonial, judicial and moral—but to fulfil it. He came to give full and perfect obedience to every part of it, to accomplish all that the Prophets had predicted of the Messiah and to fill out the reality of which the Old Testament forms were simply accurate but shadowy copies. With the fulfilling of the ceremonial and judicial elements of the law, there was no longer any need for them in their original forms, for those forms had been heightened and intensified.

The moral element, the perpetual governing principle of man's relationship to God and to his fellow man (which includes, as we have seen, the keeping of a sabbath) is also fulfilled by being written on the hearts of God's people (Hebrews 10:16 *cf* Galatians 5:16; Romans 8:3-4; 13:10). This involves a similar heightening and intensifying process. Note, for example, how the Lord drives not merely the external forms but the inward realities into the souls of men in Matthew 5:21-30, where he consistently heightens and internalises the realities of the Ten Commandments. Sinclair Ferguson identifies several elements of this fulfilling of the Law by Christ: in his doctrine and teaching; in his deeds and lifestyle; in his death, and in his disciples.[8] The Lord's fulfilment of the law means that the moral law becomes an active principle rather than a dry code. It is the Spirit-inscribed, heart-etched rule for holy living which delights our Father in heaven.

Perpetuated in his resurrection

The resurrection of Christ was the seal of God's approval, and the great manifestation of his Son's triumph over sin and death. The resurrection made no change to the purpose of the Sabbath. However, those realities did alter the day of its celebration. It is generally accepted that Christ died on a Friday, and (using inclusive counting) spent three days in the tomb, rising again on the first day. He invested that day with a particular significance by appearing on it repeatedly (John 20:19, 26—counting eight days, including the 'first day' of v19, brings us back to the first day). The church began to call it "the Lord's day" (Revelation 1:10). The principle was established at creation and affirmed in the great lawgiving dependent on the redemption from Egypt. Then the great day of re-creation and redemption came, the day of our Lord's rising from the dead. This day was, by the Lord and his church, adopted immediately as the new, divinely instituted day of worship. Jonathan Edwards, so beloved of many modern conservative evangelicals, is robust at this point. He marshals numerous strands of evidence as to how we move from a Saturday to a Sunday observance, but central among them is this:

> The sabbath was a day of rejoicing; for it was kept in commemoration of God's glorious and gracious works of creation and the redemption out of Egypt. Therefore we are directed to call the sabbath a delight. But it is not a proper day for the church, Christ's spouse, to rejoice, when Christ the bridegroom lies buried in the grave, as Christ says, Matt. 9:15. "That the children of the bride-chamber cannot mourn, while the bridegroom is with them. But the time will come, when the bridegroom shall be taken from them; then shall they mourn."--While Christ was holden under the chains of death, then the bridegroom was taken from them; then it was a proper time for the spouse to mourn and not rejoice. But when Christ rose again, then it was a day of joy, because we are begotten again to a living hope, by the resurrection of Jesus Christ from the dead.[9]

Edwards, with many others, wants to emphasise that just as the redemption of Israel produced its day of rest, so the redemption of a spiritual nation also produced a day of rest. A divine act and pattern had established the principle at the beginning of the world. A divine act and pattern had renewed the provision in connection with a shadowy redemption. So a similar divine act and pattern ushered in its new covenant form: "on this day both God the Father and God the Son, respectively, did rest from their own proper work, and by their precept and pattern command it and commend it for a stated rest to the church of God for ever."[10]

Life in the Spirit

The Lord's day is a celebration of the resurrection. It is the commemoration of Christ's purchase of his people, and the winning of our new covenant blessings in his victory over sin and death. Furthermore, the Day of Pentecost seems to have occurred on the first day of the week.[11] The Spirit of God was poured out upon the church on the Lord's day, the risen Lord's victory gift to his people. From the earliest days of the church, God's people have delighted in this truth:

> But Sunday is the day on which we all hold our common assembly, because it is the first day on which God, having wrought a change in the darkness and

matter, made the world; and Jesus Christ our Saviour on the same day rose from the dead.[12]

Perhaps more than anything else, it is the day of resurrection that persuades us of the change of the day of celebration from the seventh day of the week to the first. Richard Sibbes says,

> He rose on that day which was ever after, and well may still be, called the Lord's day; for a new world began with his rising, therefore a new Sabbath. Saint John saith, 'I was in the Spirit upon the Lord's day,' Rev. 1:10. If a man be ever in the Spirit, it is upon the Lord's day, when the Lord of the day doth honour his people, giving them to enjoy his ordinances, and joining effectually with them, maketh them full of the Spirit, and raiseth up our dead hearts after him.[13]

There is at least a possibility that the Israelite nation dated their Sabbath observance from the day of redemption, the original seventh day perhaps having been swallowed up during the period of Egyptian slavery. When the Lord rises, everything is made new. The commandment itself must remain in its essential substance, but it can be fully refreshed. It is brought to its final form outside the new heavens and the new earth in and by God the Son himself. He is not only the Legislator of the day but its very Originator, as much under the New Covenant as the Old:

As God, in the character of Creator, ordained a day to be kept in honour of his resting from his work, so it seems but natural, that when he appears in the character of Redeemer, and rests from an infinitely greater work, than that of creation, a day should be kept in honour of that glorious event.[14]

In the language of Daniel Wilson,

What more appropriate than the Lord's Day, to mark the authority of "the Lord of the Sabbath?" "If one greater than the temple be here," what more becoming than that the worship of the New Testament temple should follow his resurrection? If as "the Father worketh hitherto, so he works," what more natural than that he should display his power in making the Sabbath his own, working on it his deeds of mercy and grace, and fixing it in his own kingdom as a trophy of his resurrection?[15]

Perpetuated by the witness of the New Testament

To think of the Lord's day Sabbath as an Old Testament teaching is to ignore the constant and consistent testimony of the New Testament. We will consider some of the particulars below. My point here is simply that it is clearly woven into the New Testament. The range and depth of direct New Testament references gives the lie to the idea that this is an Old Testament issue. For example, it is addressed repeatedly in the Gospels: in Matthew 12:1-14; in Mark 2:23-3.6; in Luke 6:1-11, 13:10-17 and 14:1-6; in John 5:1-18 and 7:20-24. It is, as we shall see, in Hebrews 4:1-10 and elsewhere. Not only are the Gospels full of it, but the rest of the New Testament assumes it, refers to it very naturally and consistently and—in addition to its direct references— alludes to it and builds on it in many other respects, as we shall now see.

OBSERVED BY THE NEW TESTAMENT CHURCH

This is very clear in the Scriptures. It is the particular sphere in which the New Testament witness to a continuing day of rest is seen. The New Testament church, in its early days, was composed almost exclusively of converted Jews. That church readily adopted the day of the Lord's resurrection as its continuing Sabbath. The seamlessness of that transition suggests that many or all of those believing Jews realised the significance of what they were doing and why they were doing it. Granted, not all did. These issues were dealt with, primarily by Paul, and we will consider that later.

Nevertheless, we find this pattern of observing the first day established from the earliest days of the life of the church. Luke tells us in Acts 20:7 that it was the first day of the week, the day of Christ's resurrection, the day when the disciples came together and on which fell the significant bulk of his post-resurrection appearances. In 1 Corinthians 16:2 the first day of the week is the natural day on which the church as a corporate body is to act. It is regarded as the proper day for public worship.

At the end of his long life, when the beloved John comes to communicate to the churches the revelation given by Christ Jesus, it is no accident that he receives it on "the Lord's day" (Revelation 1:10). Note that John does not need to explain this reference to any of the churches to whom he writes. That knowledge is safely assumed. The entire apostolic church recognises and sanctions the first day of the week as the one hallowed by the Lord's rising from the dead. It is therefore the day not just best suited or most appropriate but divinely appointed to be set apart for the worship of the Triune God.

Gathered for worship

No less significant are some of the implications of that principle of worship, especially for the corporate people of God. Although there may be some differences of opinion with regard to the detail, no doubt we all long for a fuller expression of the unity of all the Lord's people, often defined as 'the church universal.' The universal church is the whole number of Christ's redeemed people across all time and from every place. Historically, the concept of the universal church has, at points, been threatened because of the apparent absence of any assembly of this church. A church is, by definition, an assembly, goes the argument. If we envision the church universal, it must assemble. Otherwise, by definition, it is no church. If the church universal does not assemble, then there is no universal church, only the local church, for only the local church can assemble and thereby be a true church.[16] A Baptist pastor and theologian in the United States, Greg Nichols, suggests the following solution to the proposed problem. Even if you do not admit the dilemma, or fully embrace the solution, his treatment can be genuinely helpful in our notion of the worship of the church. He begins with an Old Testament concept called the *qahal*. This is the proper name for the gathering of the congregation of Israel for the purposes of worship and warfare. His treatment of this aspect is lengthy, but worth considering carefully. Dr Nichols writes as follows:

> The crux is identifying the focal point of the gathering of the universal church. Here the continuity with the qahal of Jehovah, and the clear biblical teaching on the gathering point of Jehovah's assembly, shows us the way.
>
> Jehovah's assembly was, by divine mandate, directed to gather in God's special presence (or sacramental) presence. God is omnipresent, true, but God is also especially present, in accordance with His own sovereign will and appointment. The males were to appear 'before him' three times a year. They

congregated 'in the place where he chose to dwell.' In the wilderness this was the tabernacle. In the land it became Jerusalem, Zion, the Temple. The focal point of the gathering of the assembly of Jehovah was the special presence of Jehovah.

This has not changed. The universal assembly of Jesus Christ comes to this same focal point or meeting place, by divine mandate. The crucial factor is that God's special presence is no longer restricted to one geographical location. Marvelously and mysteriously, this one and the same special presence is now manifested and located in a multitude of places at the same time. Each local assembly is a temple of God. Each assembly wherever and whenever it assembles enters this special presence of God – the same presence, and therefore the same place.

God has also appointed a weekly day on which the entire catholic assembly shall enter into his special presence together. Every week, on the Lord's day, the entire church universal assembles and meets in the one special presence of God. This began at Pentecost, when, for the first time, the special presence of God, the Holy Spirit, filled the new temple in Jerusalem made of Christ's disciples and vacated the temple made of stones. This has continued every Lord's day since then for almost 2000 years. Unless we are prepared to deny that the special presence of God is one or real, we cannot deny the weekly gathering of the universal church.

Try to imagine, from God's vantage point, the

universal church meeting in his presence on the Lord's day. At dawn in the Pacific, as the day begins, the congregations in the islands gather for worship in his presence. God hears their united praises. Immediately numerous congregations in New Zealand, then in Korea, Japan, Australia enter that same presence as God's praises sweep across Asia. Many tongues in China, Indonesia, Pakistan, Tibet, join them there in his presence and utter the honors of his name. India joins the chorus. Then a relatively few voices in the Middle East join too. A brief lull in the volume of God's praise occurs as the sun sweeps the Arab lands marred by Moslem darkness and the northern part of Asia suppressed by communist oppression. But even across Russia praises are being sung to God as congregations secretly come into God's presence. Then God's praise erupts as Africa and Europe enter the assembly. An intense shrill climbs to heaven. Finally, beginning in Brazil, the Americas join the chorus. All over America voices rise to heaven. Here is perhaps, at least in terms of numbers, the loudest burst of praise to God throughout this day of assembly in God's presence. Volume, however, is not the best measure of quality, but sincerity of heart.

Then the praises of God again cross the sea. They ebb out over the Pacific and come to a close in the islands where they began 24 hours before.

This is the way the universal church enters God's special presence today, 2000 years after Christ came. The glory of God truly has filled the earth as the waters cover the sea. This really happens, every Lord's day. We do not often think of it. Perhaps we should contemplate more frequently the praises of the entire catholic church of which we are but a tiny part.

Now it was not always so. The gathering of the universal church into God's presence began in a very modest fashion. There was silence on a Lord's day until the sun reached the Middle East. There the church in Jerusalem, beginning at Pentecost, gathered on the Lord's Day to bring God praises. Silence was heard over the rest of the earth. In a few years, God's praises were being sung on the Lord's day all over Judea. They soon spread to Antioch, and Gentile voices joined the chorus. By the end of the first century God's praises were being sung all across Europe and in Northern Africa. The church soon formed a ring around the Mediterranean. God's praises also moved eastward into India. So it continued for many centuries. The day began with silence, a burst of praise arose in Europe, and the day ended in silence. But then God moved again to spread his church. He stirred up the hearts of his servants, and through a new wave of missionary effort God's praises penetrated every continent to reach the level attained today. 'To him be the glory, in Christ Jesus and in his church, through all generations for ever. Amen!'

In summary, the universal church gathers both in this age, on the Lord's day, and in the age to come on the Day of the Lord, when Jesus comes in glory. The focal point of its gathering is the special presence of the living God.[17]

This underlines the significance of the holy labour in which we engage on the Lord's day. If we want to express our unity with all God's true people, one of the most expressive and significant ways in which we can do so is to gather with them in the special presence of God on the day which he has appointed.

Spiritual warfare, spiritual worship

There are plain implications also for the local church. As we have seen, for the Christians of the apostolic and post-apostolic periods it was the day on which they naturally gathered to conduct their corporate business: "the day on which we all hold our common assembly."[18] The key elements of that business, like the Old Testament *qahal*, are warfare (we should, of course, underline that this is spiritual warfare) and worship.

There are many other principles that Scripture provides dealing with the life of a local church. This one underlines that the weekly gathering of a particular body of Christians on the Lord's day ought to be, and ought to be seen and felt to be, one of our greatest privileges (Hebrews 10:24-25). By such gatherings, Christians express their unity with the church universal. They express their particular, local unity, and foster it in the expression of their love for the Lord Jesus Christ and for each other. They join their hearts and voices in praise to their God and Saviour. Their hopes, their fears, their concerns, their needs, and their joys are shared and corporately expressed. The members of the Lord's body can play out their particular functions in relation one to another largely but not exclusively on the Lord's day. Appreciating this gives us good grounds to explain to church members, visitors, and our own families (especially our children) why we do these things. It is why we take our Sunday gatherings so seriously. The weekly congregation of God's people is one of our greatest privileges as well as one of our greatest responsibilities. The public worship of the gathered church is closest on earth we get to heaven. Sutcliff says it is

> the employ of heaven, begun on earth.—Recollect the benefit you have enjoyed. Have not you reason to be thankful for the sabbath? Have not some of the sweetest seasons you ever enjoyed, been on this happy day? Pleasant were the hours when you retired from the world, and enjoyed your God.[19]

Despite that, we live in an age where church attendance is falling off at an ever-increasing rate. Even within evangelical circles the prospect of attending church more than once on Sunday is considered, at best, unnecessary. For some, it is viewed as extreme, even fanatical and legalistic. Being with God's people in God's presence on God's day seems to come far down the list of priorities.

On the contrary, the Christian ought to have no greater pleasure and can have few greater benefits than to gather with the people of God in the presence of God. To miss such opportunities (where not providentially hindered) – or, even worse, to neglect or avoid them – is contrary to the expressed will of God for his people. Furthermore, it exposes the mistaken believer not only in the short term, but also and especially in the long term, to great danger. Do you remember the example of David? David sinned by committing adultery and murder (2Sam 11). The sorry tale began because he was not where he ought to have been when he ought to have been there (*i.e.* leading Israel gathered for war as part of the *qahal*). This at least points to the danger in which an individual Christian can place himself by absenteeism. He exposes and damages himself by his absence, because he is not in the place of responsibility and safety. He endangers his brothers and sisters in Christ, because he is not there to serve them. He dishonours the God of his salvation, because he is not where he should be, among God's people, serving his Lord and praising the name of God.

ENJOYED IN GLORY

In this section we have to deal with some technical language and some significant ideas, but do not let that put you off. These are rich, biblical concepts. If we have not heard of them before, or been scared away from considering them, now is a good time to get to grips with them.

The Lord's day was and remains a typical foreshadowing of what is called our eschatological rest. Eschatology has to do with 'the last things'—death, judgement, heaven and hell. In this respect, the Lord's day looks and points forward to these last things. There is a fundamentally anticipatory aspect to the purpose of the Sabbath day.

The various blessings of salvation and redemption, such as life, freedom, peace, and rest that we have in the Lord Jesus Christ, come to their final and fullest expression in the eschatological realm, in the new heavens and the new earth. For this reason, says one scholar, "Sabbath rest ... is ultimately related to and characterizes the order of the Spirit."[20] (He bases this on a thorough exposition of 1 Corinthians 15:44-49.) This simply means that the supreme expression and enjoyment of this day of rest belongs to the new creation.

From the beginning, Adam's probationary period in the Garden of Eden—the period when he was under God's command not to eat from the tree of the knowledge of good and evil—had a purpose. This probationary period was laying a foundation in Adam's experience and action for something greater and more lasting to come.

In other words, the "weekly cycle impressed on Adam that he, together with the created order as a whole, was moving toward a goal, a nothing-less-than eschatological culmination."[21] The weekly cycle of work and rest was sending a message to Adam: this is not the end. There is more to come!

A rest to come

In the light of this typical and anticipatory character, the Lord's day is a day to pause. We are called to rest and reflect, to consider "the ultimate outcome of history," the point at which the present order of things will be entirely transformed into something truly Spiritual—something entirely and sweetly under the characteristic influence of the Holy Spirit. It is a time to consider our life and calling. We are supposed to look around us on the Lord's day, look back over the previous six days of labour, and think about it all in the light of eternity.[22]

When the Bible speaks about heaven, it is represented and comprehended most often under the figure of rest (*e.g.* Hebrews 4:1-13). The most appropriate representation of the permanence and perfection of this spiritual rest to come is our present rest. Rest now points ahead to that state where the work characteristic of this age is unnecessary, because nothing remains to be perfected. It symbolises the full and final realisation of everything for which the Christian is waiting.[23] In other words, we might ask the question, "What is the best way to get a taste of the heavenly rest?" The short answer? "Earthly rest!"

These are deep and sweet truths that require some complicated language. I hope, though, that you can feel the momentum of thought. The rest that we enjoy here and now, every Lord's day, in our natural bodies in this world, is a foretaste of the everlasting rest we shall enjoy in bodies like that of the risen Jesus in the world to come. Our rest remains, "not only in terms of the Sabbath rest of Christ (to be entered by his people by faith) but also in terms of an earthly Sabbath day which points to it (to be observed by his New Covenant people)." The Lord's day is "a Christian Sabbath to be observed by God's New Covenant people in remembrance of the great redemptive work of Christ in securing for us an inheritance in his Sabbath rest, and as a pledge of our entering that rest."[24]

If this is so, we must ask how those who find the Lord's day a burden and an imposition now could possibly enjoy heaven to come? That is not a cheap jibe, but a serious concern. The writer to the Hebrews makes very plain that there is a rest still to come. His principle is the same as ours: he goes back to creation (Hebrews 4:4). The rest is already begun in the believer, in our experience of salvation and the day of its celebration. However, that experience of rest has a clear eschatological aim—even now, it is not of this creation (Hebrews 9:11). The Christian looks forward to a heavenly country, to the consummation of the good things that we already know in essence, to the place where we shall know them in their fullness. They belong to us now in Christ, and do so completely, and we begin to enjoy them now as well. However, they will not be fully tasted until we sit down with him in heaven. The worship of God is realised in glory in a way that it is not now. The revelation of Christ given to John is given on the Lord's day, and culminates in the consummation of the Sabbath rest, in its fullest, truest, and final sense. Do you know the picture of heaven's activity in Revelation 7:

> After these things I looked, and behold, a great multitude which no one could number, of all nations, tribes, peoples, and tongues, standing before the throne and before the Lamb, clothed with white robes, with palm branches in their hands, and crying out with a loud voice, saying, "Salvation belongs to our God who sits on the throne, and to the Lamb!" All the angels stood around the throne and the elders and the four living creatures, and fell on their faces before the throne and worshipped God, saying: "Amen! Blessing and glory and wisdom, Thanksgiving and honour and power and might, Be to our God forever and ever. Amen."
>
> — REVELATION 7:9–12

It is a sweet picture of a perpetual Sabbath, granted to those who rest from their labours (Revelation 14:13), and whose eternity is spent in unalloyed adoration of God in Christ (Revelation 21:1-7, 22-3).

OBJECTIONS CONSIDERED

Before we move on, we must consider some significant objections. There are at least three New Testament passages to look at. These may, at first glance, appear (at best) to undermine or even (at worst) flatly to contradict all we have been saying about the Lord's day. These passages are Romans 14.1-8, Galatians 4.8-11, and Colossians 2.11-23. In each of these passages there are warnings against what we can summarise as 'the observance of days'.

The observance of days?

To the Romans, Paul writes that "one person esteems one day above another, another esteems each[25] day. Let each be fully convinced in his own mind. He who observes the day, observes it to the Lord; and he who does not observe the day, to the Lord he does not observe it.[26] He who eats, eats to the Lord, for he gives God thanks; and he who does not eat, to the Lord he does not eat, and gives God thanks."

He warns the Galatians against turning back to weak and beggarly elements, which is a desire to return to bondage. He uses as an example of such slavery the observing of "days and months and seasons and years."

To the Colossians he seems, perhaps, most clear. Reasoning from the real triumph of Christ, he urges the Colossians to "let no one judge you in food or in drink, or regarding a festival or a new moon or sabbaths." He further asks, "why, as though living in the world, do you submit yourselves to regulations—'do not touch, do not taste, do not handle,' which all concern things which perish with the using—according to the commandments and doctrines of men? These things have an appearance of wisdom in self-imposed religion, false humility, and neglect of the body, but are of no value against the indulgence of the flesh."

How are we to interpret these things in the light of the other matters we have been considering? Does the letter to the Romans teach us that observing anything that could be considered a sabbath is a matter of liberty of conscience? Does it mean that one can observe it, but that others are free not to, as long as all do it 'to the Lord'? Does Paul not condemn the Sabbath as part of mere legal, outward ceremony? Should it not be abandoned with the rest of the Mosaic code? Are we not, if we observe the Lord's day, being defrauded, and returning to bondage?

Fighting for freedom

To understand and to answer these questions, we need to put them in the context in which Paul laboured, and in which these letters were written. Paul was the apostle to the Gentiles. He struggled for much (if not all) of his life with attempts by some confused Jewish converts and some Judaizing professors of religion (not true Christians at all) to reintroduce elements of the Jewish law into the life of the new covenant church. Such false teachers sought to bind the Gentile element in the church to these things as a means of satisfying God, as if we could acquire salvation by means of our own obedience.

Paul's teaching on matters of conscience usually touches on these issues (or those of pagan Gentiles being emancipated from their idolatry). He wanted to guard against what we often call Pharisaism—basically a kind of 'works righteousness.' This is the idea, which we have already mentioned, that you can win and keep God's favour by being good enough. Paul himself had been delivered from that kind of life. Now he saw it creeping back into the church, often introduced under a Christian guise. At the same time, he wanted to recognise the tender consciences of some Jewish converts who still held, as Jews, to the habits and traditions of Judaism.

The Jews had been expelled from the Roman capital by Claudius in 49AD. This would have included the believers who may have founded the church after hearing Peter preach the gospel at Pentecost (Acts 2:10). When Paul wrote, these Jews—Christians as well as others— had been allowed to return. In their absence, the Gentile Christians, without feeling any constraint from Jewish backgrounds, would have continued to build the church. When the Christian Jews (who had probably planted the church) returned, they would have found new faces, new leaders, and new practices. Many of the habits and expectations of Judaism, not to mention any additions and accretions, were probably long gone. Those of tender conscience —the weaker brethren who had not yet grasped the fullness of their emancipation from the shadows of ceremony—might have been offended at this. Some would have continued observing the Jewish calendar and feasts. Into this context Paul writes, seeking to promote, among other things, the unity and peace of a cosmopolitan church.

The churches in Galatia were dealing with people who perverted or twisted the gospel (Galatians 1:7). These false teachers were promoting the works of the law as the means of attaining that which comes only by the hearing of faith (Galatians 3:2). Paul knew and taught that, in truth, "no-one is justified by the law in the sight of God" (Galatians 3:11), not even believing Abraham, the father of the faithful.

In Colosse, heresy had crept in. The heretics were devaluing Christ as the way by which a sinner entered into and enjoyed a relationship with God. They were, in essence, telling Christians that Christ was not quite enough, and so seeking to add to him. They offered alternatives or at least supplements to knowing the Lord Jesus as a way to advance as Christians. Paul set out to defend Christ's supremacy against those who would claim that, in order to know the fullness of Christian experience, something beyond Christ was needed. Apparently, one element that was being introduced as part of this need was a legalistic observance of human commandment and doctrine.

The unifying feature of these passages is this question of days. In the letter to the Romans, the issue is more legitimate though confused; in Galatians and Colossians, it is heretical and dangerous. In Rome, there are those who observe a certain day or number of days as part of their relationship with God. In Galatia and Colosse, there are those who promote as a necessary addition to Christ the religious observance of a certain day or number of days.

A question of days

We need to understand Paul's response. It is perhaps simplest to restrict ourselves to the basic problem in the Galatian and Colossian fields, although Paul's attitude will cast light on the Romans issue. Paul is struggling against the emergence and penetration into the church of a Judaizing element. He battles the establishment of a sort of 'Christian pharisaism,' if two such contradictory terms can be brought together. Believers who had never been subject to the Mosaic requirements of ceremonies, and never needed to be, were being urged to turn back to and come under those requirements as a means of obtaining or maintaining salvation. In the face of such teachings Paul declares boldly that "the substance is of Christ"—the fleshing out of the ceremonial shadows has been accomplished in him, and there is no longer a need for those things.

Paul knew what it was to be all things to all men (1 Corinthians 9:22). That he himself was freed from the law in this sense is evident. He could observe the

Sabbath as a Jew, and he used it for the sake of preaching the gospel (see Acts 13:14, 42-44, where even the Gentiles proceed in accordance with the Jewish pattern). However, Paul felt under no obligation to subscribe to Jewish ceremonial law. He did so (*e.g.* Acts 21) when it was necessary to live at peace with all men, but the ceremonial law did not bind him. Note, though, that throughout the Acts of the Apostles the Lord's people observe the first day of the week, and there is Paul taking his part as an apostolic preacher (Acts 20:7)!

Everywhere, Paul strives against the intrusion of Jewish practice into the church of Christ on such a basis as this. He even withstands Peter to his face (Galatians 2:11) when that good and godly man is temporarily led astray, with other Jews, by these Judaizers. In Galatians and Colossians, it is the Judaizers about whom Paul writes, and against whom he is struggling. They are seeking to introduce into the church obsolete elements of the ceremonial and judicial law that are no longer binding on the Christian conscience. This included the observance of days that were established as part of the Jewish calendar.

With those Jews who are gradually coming to terms with their emancipation from this law Paul is always gracious and tender (*e.g.* Romans 14, Acts 15). With anyone who would reintroduce it and insist upon it as the basis of man's acceptance with God, Paul is utterly and rightly merciless.

Paul is talking, then, about Jewish sabbaths (and other days and seasons)—parts of the now-obsolete ceremonial and judicial law. He is not talking about the Lord's day, which he himself observed (Acts 20:7). The apostle Paul, with his great grasp of the truth, and his sure insight into the perpetuity of the creation ordinances and the moral law, never put away the moral law, which is perpetually binding. We would no more expect to find Paul promoting adultery as part of Christian liberty than we should expect to find him ignoring the claims of the Lord's day. The Sabbath principle, adopted by the new covenant church as the Lord's day, was never—as we have seen—part of the ceremonial or judicial law (although at times coloured by it). It was never a mere Jewish custom. It was a creation ordinance. It was restored to its rightful place through the redemption of Israel from Egypt. It was clearly revealed in the moral law, that law which is now written on the heart and mind of every believer (Hebrews 10:16).

The danger of legalism

Is there a danger of legalism in our observance of a new covenant day of rest? Of course, just as there is a danger of legalism when any part of our obedience as Christians is ripped out of its proper place and elevated to a role it was never intended to have. But legalism is the idea that we can get right or stay right with God by our own obedience. It is *not* a handy description for an attitude of principled obedience to the God of our salvation!

The liberty Paul claims in this instance is liberty for

the weaker brethren. It is freedom for those who are coming to a full knowledge of their new freedom in Christ. It is freedom to observe certain of the patterns of their forefathers, so long as they attribute to them nothing with regard to their salvation. Against those who would re-introduce these days (and foods, and create new commandments, and so on) as part of Christian duty, Paul shows that those things are a return to bondage. Paul's appreciation and commendation of liberty with regard to days does not allow the new covenant church to begin pursuing emancipation from the moral law – not from any part of it, including the fourth commandment! If we do so in the mistaken pursuit of liberty then we have gone too far. We have gone beyond Scripture. Our Saviour, as Lord of the Sabbath, has returned this day to us. It is for us a commemoration of his resurrection, with its proper form and function restored, renewed, and even expanded. It is not something to be put aside.

Such then, are the biblical data which demonstrate the Sabbath to be a perpetual ordinance. The principle should be recognised and adopted under Christ as the Lord's day, the first day of the week (our Sunday), on which he rose from the dead. It is, in itself, a foretaste of the heavenly rest to come.

But we must move on. Having established the fact that God lays claim to the first day of every week, we must ask, "Why does he do this?" For what purpose does God claim our time and energies in this way?

2

THE PURPOSE OF THE LORD'S DAY

We should consider the significance always attached by our Creator and Redeemer to Sabbath observance. Our starting point for this is Exodus 31:14. There, the Lord says, "You shall keep the Sabbath, therefore, for it is holy to you. Everyone who profanes it shall surely be put to death; for whoever does any work on it, that person shall be cut off from among his people."

Here God contrasts keeping the Sabbath holy (its sanctification) with profaning the Sabbath (despising or desecrating it). The Old Testament speaks of profaning God's name, his holy sanctuary, Jerusalem, sabbaths, offerings and sacrifices. It also speaks of profane priests and people. The word has to do with the contravention of God's will, acting in a way which offends and insults his holiness. When something that God has called to be or designated holy is profaned, it is an assault on the value system that the Lord God righteously and legitimately imposes as Creator and as Redeemer.

God's values

The profaning of the Sabbath is mentioned in Exodus 31:14. It is mentioned in Isaiah 56:2 and 6 (part of the sequence that includes Isaiah 58, and thus part of the backdrop to it). It is mentioned in Ezekiel 20:13, 16, 21, and 24, 22:8, and 23:38. It is mentioned in Nehemiah 13:17-18.

It is one of God's regular complaints against Israel that they desecrate the day that he has given to them for specific purposes. Throughout the books of Moses this creation ordinance and the fourth commandment underpin or are built upon by the ceremonial and judicial law (which the Pharisees would later abuse in their own way). Throughout the Old Testament we find that the Jews profoundly misunderstood or abused the Sabbath. This profaning, with regard to the Sabbath, is essentially a rejection of the divine authority of God. It is an attempt to throw off his lordship over our time and our labour, and asserting would-be human autonomy[1] in its place. The divine value system is assaulted: God establishes the day for a holy purpose, but man rebels against God's purpose.

We need to see profaning the Sabbath as God sees it: rebellion. God's faultless 'memory' records that the sign of the Sabbath, the sign that he was the Lord, was constantly defiled by Israel (Ezekiel 20). The profaning of the Sabbaths was a result of idolatry. It was the expression of Israel's despising of God's statutes. It became the site of a pitched battle for the soul of the nation. As such, it was just cause for God's fury, for his anger to be poured out. It was and remains expressive of the greater battle for the allegiance of man to God rather than idols (of which the greatest is often self). The Sabbath principle is, in this regard, a key index of godliness, because it exalts God rather than self.

Nehemiah, Amos, and us

Nehemiah (who in Nehemiah 9:14 considers the making known of a "holy Sabbath" to be one of Israel's great covenant privileges) undertakes a thorough reformation in Israel. That reformation includes specific and detailed reference to Sabbath observance (Nehemiah 10:31). In Nehemiah 13:15-22, the use of the Sabbath for trade is a great grief to this righteous man, and he vigorously fights against it, speaking of the profanation of the Sabbath as positively evil. Regarding the fact and nature of the people's work on the Jewish Sabbath, he asks, "Did not your fathers do thus, and did not our God bring all this disaster on us and on this city? Yet you bring added wrath on Israel by profaning the Sabbath" (Nehemiah 13:18). Defiling the Sabbath was characteristic of the sin of Isaiah's day (Isaiah 56:2, 6). God's call to a proper observance of the Sabbath is part of Isaiah's message to the sinful nation. Jeremiah is sent by God to identify the sins of the nation with regard to the Sabbath (Jeremiah

17:19-27). He promises, in God's name, blessings for specific obedience in this regard, and awful destruction if they will not heed God's word.

In Amos' day the Jews complained against what they saw as an unreasonable imposition. The Sabbath and other holy days prevented them from doing their pleasure, and they complained: "When will the New Moon be past, that we may sell grain? And the Sabbath, that we may trade our wheat?" (Amos 8.5). God's demands were getting in the way of their desires.

These same attitudes and sins are prominent in our own day and age. We should make our assessment in the light of what we have seen about the additional significance attached to the Lord's day through the resurrection of Christ. Given all this, what should we make of the casual ignorance and looseness which characterises not just the world, but also the professing church of Christ? Could it be grounds for God's continued displeasure? He has clearly established a definite purpose for this day. We are no less culpable—given the light we have, much more so—for our continued disobedience to God's desires for us. To profane the Sabbath, in the sense of despising the day God gives, is still rebellion. It still grieves the Lord.

There is a pitched battle being fought for the soul of the church, and the Lord's day remains one of the more potent symbols of that fight. Who has authority over our time and energy? The two points of assault are precisely what they were in the days of Nehemiah and Amos: erosion from within and assault from without. In

Nehemiah's time the people of God were going about their ordinary business on the Sabbath. The people of the world were encouraging them in it. Today's "men of Tyre" have made inroads into the practice of the Lord's day. Today's people of God are aping the world and adopting their practices. Often, we are erecting no principled defence against the attack, but simply succumbing to it.

God has given us good grounds, throughout his Word, to conduct a Nehemiah-like reformation of our attitude to and use of the Lord's day, and to bring our heart attitudes, and our practice, back into line with the purposes which follow.

God's intention

We see that the Lord our God takes with awesome seriousness the proper observance of the Sabbath day. It is given for a purpose, and that purpose is not to be put aside: the day is not to be profaned. I hope you can appreciate why God ordained a Sabbath—the principle of the Lord's day, which we have been considering, especially its typical and anticipatory function (that it is, at a fundamental level, a foretaste of heaven). When we grasp this, we gain a foundation to appreciate the purpose of the new covenant day of rest, and the danger of its not being appreciated. Not entering into 'the rest' is the most appalling judgement to be imagined. Neglecting its foretaste is a tragedy. We need to see why the Sabbath is there in principle. In that way, we can appreciate the richness of God's designs for it, the care he takes to prescribe the way in which it is to be employed, and his concern over its abuse.

To consider God's underlying purposes for the Lord's day, we turn our attention to one of the clearest and most beautiful passages dealing with the whole issue of Sabbath worship, Isaiah 58.13-14:

> If you turn away your foot from the Sabbath,
> From doing your pleasure on my holy day,
> And call the Sabbath a delight,
> The holy day of the Lord honourable,
> And shall honour him, not doing your own ways,
> Nor finding your own pleasure,
> Nor speaking your own words,
> Then you shall delight yourself in the Lord;
> And I will cause you to ride on the high hills of the earth,
> And feed you with the heritage of Jacob your father.
> The mouth of the Lord has spoken.

For the sake of simplicity, I want to deal with these verses under three headings. They will help identify that which lies at the centre of the purpose of our one day set aside by and for the Lord our God. The first two purposes are Godward. The third is manward. Each is God-centred. It is a balance worth remembering.

THE GLORY OF GOD

This day was a day to be set apart ('sanctified') to honour God and to glorify him. Pre-eminently, it is God's day. It is the day on which he requires man to give him, in a particular sense, the honour and glory due to his name. It was set apart by God himself, and therefore it is to be observed in a manner pleasing to him *i.e.* in the manner which he has indicated will please him. We are not left scratching our heads as to what will glorify and honour God. He himself has told us.

What Isaiah commends is an utterly unworldly perspective on the Sabbath, one that is truly contrary to the mind of sinful man. By nature, we place ourselves at the centre of our time and our attentions. Isaiah says that this should be a day on which we look entirely out of and away from ourselves. We are to enjoy the exquisite delights to be found in one infinitely more delightful than we are ourselves. When our Lord tells us that the Sabbath was made for man, not man for the Sabbath (Mark 2:27), he is not suggesting that it is simply a man-centred day. Remember, the Sabbath was made for man before he fell, when he enjoyed unbroken communion with God. It was made for man to glorify God, and only a biblical view of the chief end or purpose of man[2] can appreciate that the Sabbath was made for man to accomplish his chief end. It was given to man to do what he was created to do: to put God, and not himself, at the centre of his life.

Honouring self

Observe the primary spheres in which the man-centred perspective operates: our own ways, our own pleasures, and our own words. All these are in contrast to honouring God. The scholar E. J. Young characterises these three spheres concisely. A way is a course of conduct, and "our own way" refers to all courses and actions that men choose in preference to the commands of God. Some of these may be legitimate in themselves in their proper place, but their proper place is not the Sabbath. "Our own pleasure" consists in finding one's own pleasure in distinction from what pleases God. "Our own words" is probably a reference to idle and vain talk, in which God is forgotten or ignored. What is mentioned tends to draw the heart away from God to the consideration of one's own occupations. This is wrong conduct on the holy sabbath.[3]

This is man-centred activity, where the creature usurps the place of the Creator and becomes the focus of his own attention. By contrast, we ought to honour God in honouring his day. See how closely the two concepts are bound up. There seems almost a degree of identification. We honour God by doing what he commands. If we fail to do what he commands by honouring his day, we are in that very act dishonouring God. It is not sufficient merely to acknowledge the purposes of the Lord's day. We must act upon them. Note that mere observation is not honouring God on his Sabbath. There is nothing honouring to God about going through the motions of sabbatarianism, without engaging in the work with our hearts, whether we think of life in the shadows of the old covenant or the light of the new. We can do all the right things in the right places, but if we lack the right motive, we actually bring wrath upon ourselves.

Honouring God

We honour God, then, in the simple act of willing obedience with regard to his Sabbath day. However, as we have seen, it is the resurrection day, and nothing could be more natural than to take such an opportunity to glorify God for all his wondrous works. The hymn-writer John Monsell writes of Sunday:

> *'Tis His day of resurrection,*
> *Let us rise and keep the feast.*
>
> *Christ is risen! Hallelujah!*
> *Risen our victorious Head!*
> *Sing His praises! Hallelujah!*
> *Christ is risen from the dead.*

Israel of old looked back on the redemption from Egypt with praises welling from their hearts through their mouths (*e.g.* Psalm 78, 95, 106). So ought the new covenant Israel of God to rejoice in the God of our salvation. In the Lord Jesus Christ, far more clearly than ever before, the glorious attributes of God shine forth in splendour and beautiful harmony. The brightness of the Father's glory is seen in Jesus Christ more clearly than it was in the temple of old. God's wisdom and power are nowhere manifested as they are in "Christ and him crucified." We set out on this day to honour God. We could almost ask, given what it is that we are commemorating, how could we not?

This is our active purpose, and there is no unfairness in it. If a man gave you £700 to use, on condition only that you use £100 for him, would it be considered unreasonable? Of course not! Only the most warped sense of entitlement would say, "You gave it to me, now I can do with it what I like. You have no right to impose any obligations upon me!" No more is it unreasonable that God gives mankind seven days, of which six are bestowed on us to serve the Lord in various legitimate and appropriate ways, one only being reserved entirely for God in a particular and distinct way. It is a day to be devoted to God. Remember, it is a foretaste of heaven, a picture of which we have already considered from Revelation 7.9ff. We are to pursue, so far as we are able, the practice of the church triumphant, in accordance with the guidance laid out for us by God in Scripture for the worship of his holy name.

THE ENJOYMENT OF GOD

This is closely linked with the glory of God. Should we really consider it a hardship to spend a day honouring

God? Should it be painful to celebrate the redemptive designs and acts of our Father in heaven, in the finished work of our glorious Saviour, bestowed and applied by the Spirit of the Most High?

See how Isaiah puts it. We are to turn away from our own desires in order that we might honour the Lord. He contrasts the pursuit of our own pleasure with calling the Sabbath a delight. Is he saying that on such a day we are to turn away from everything that is pleasant? Is he suggesting that the Sabbath is to be a day of drudgery, woe, and dullness? Not in the slightest! To interpret it in this way is fundamentally to misconstrue the prophet's intention. The contrast to "your pleasure" is the idea of true and exquisite delight. God has given us a day of delight in part because "we soon disrespect that which we take no pleasure in."[4] The contrast drawn is not between pleasure and pain, between joy and misery, but between two different principles and pursuits of pleasure: the pleasure of man for man, and the pleasure of man in God.

Delight in God

When we put the day to the purposes for which God intends it, "then you shall delight yourself in the Lord" (Isaiah 58:14a). "Joy suits no man so much as a saint, and no day so much as a Sabbath."[5] Here is the true pleasure, the pleasure which far transcends our own pleasure, that lowly and pitiful pleasure from which we are to turn away. We are to delight ourselves in God. To continue the analogy from above, that £100 which we invest in the one who bestowed it upon us brings us more joy than anything else we do with the other £600.

Isaiah's warning to turn away from doing our own pleasure is a rebuke to those who would pervert the Sabbath ordinance (by merely notional or twisted observance, such as the Pharisees), as well as to those who would neglect it (*e.g.* the traders of Amos' day). Neither group is concerned with anything other than its own ends. In both instances, the focus is on self, the only difference being that one approach masquerades as religion, wearing the robes of a priest, while the other cavorts as fun and profit, dressed as the worldling.

Again, the right perspective is a fundamentally God-centred perspective. The Lord is to be placed at the centre of our time and our attentions. An old proverb informs us that someone wrapped up in themselves makes a very small package. We will always be a small package, and have small pleasures, while we remain wrapped up in ourselves. It is only when we become enraptured with God, wrapped up in him, that we shall begin to know the glorious extent of pleasure in the divine.

A foretaste of glory

Again we see the eschatological element. We will nowhere enjoy God as we will enjoy him in glory, and this Sabbath rest is a foretaste of that. This gives the lie to those who characterise heaven as a morbid, dull, and —worst of all, in their view—eternal service of worship. Such men and women have entirely missed the purpose of the Sabbath day from the beginning. They cannot see beyond forms and appearances. What they want is to do their own pleasure on the Sabbath. The delight in God which the people of God feel as they honour and enjoy him on the day he has appointed for it is alien to them. It will remain alien to them unless God translates them from the kingdom of darkness into the kingdom of life and light, the kingdom of the Son of his love. Only the redeemed can envisage or imagine the joy of having an eternity to rejoice in their Redeemer. Those who are forgiven little, the same love little. The forgiven sinner loves much, and to glorify God and to enjoy him forever becomes the very apex of happiness as they wean their minds and hearts off the world, and put on the new man, training themselves in godliness.

Worship is not meant to be a dry and sterile process, either in public or in private. This does not mean that we give ourselves up to worldly and carnal gratification, or ape the world's ideas of life and liberty and the pursuits of wicked men (John 4:24 *cf* Romans 12:1-2). True and spiritual worship delights the heart. It demands and consumes the entirety of our redeemed humanity in the glorious and God-glorifying work. Read the psalms to see the joy with which David and his fellow inspired writers worship their God and ours. In public, when the church gathers, we are all to be engaged in the singing and praying, sounding our "Amen!" with vigour. The mind and heart and will and spirit are to be engaged in the preaching and hearing of the written-down revelation of the living God of heaven and earth. In private, in reading, meditating, praying, singing, conversing with others, reviewing the truth, we are to delight ourselves in God. Sometimes that will manifest itself in the most crushing moments of abject repentance and humility, as well as a joyous lifting up by God.[6]

However, we will never know how to enjoy God in these things without effort and determination. Such pleasure does not simply drop into our laps. It requires our own application. We are to turn our feet from doing our own pleasure on the Sabbath. We are to call God's day a delight, the holy day of the Lord honourable. It is then that we shall delight ourselves in the Lord, and he then causes us to ride on the high hills of the earth. It is not dissimilar to beginning a new exercise regime. Few of us enjoy taking up jogging for example, or getting back in training for a new season of our favourite sport. It is painful at first, as we start using muscles we have not used for a while, or perhaps ever before. We are pushing ourselves beyond what have become our normal limits. As our endurance improves, and we become used to the expanded range of movement and demands imposed on our bodies, we become better at it and even begin to enjoy it. Soon those who were plodding, stumbling, sore and blistered, start flying, excelling in strength and suppleness. Thus it is with spiritual exercises. Too often our spirit is flabby, weak, and malnourished. It is not until we put our souls on a spiritual exercise regime that their endurance will improve, their capacity will develop, and true delight in worship will be more known and felt.

THE BLESSING OF MAN

We have considered our relationship to God, and this is not a one-way process. When a man, woman, or child draws near to and delights him or herself in God, that man, woman or child does not go away unchanged. God does not intend the Lord's day to leave us completely untouched. God himself has granted us the Sabbath day for the greatest blessing any one of us could hope for-- the dedicated pursuit of true communion with our Lord and our God. In Exodus 20:11 we are told that the Lord himself blessed and hallowed the day. What better indication could we have, what greater expectation can we have, than to expect God to bless us on the day he has blessed and hallowed for the purposes for which we are employing it? The Puritan, Richard Sibbes, put it this way when encouraging us to make much of the Lord's day:

> The heart of a Christian is Christ's garden, and his graces are as so many sweet spices and flowers, which his Spirit blowing upon makes them to send forth a sweet savour: therefore keep the soul open for entertainment of the Holy Ghost, for he will bring in continually fresh forces to subdue corruption, and this

most of all on the Lord's day. John was in the Spirit on the Lord's day, even in Patmos, the place of his banishment, Rev. 1:10; then the gales of the Spirit blow more strongly and sweetly.[7]

Look again at Isaiah 58:14. What happens when we delight ourselves in the Lord? Joy, victory, feasting! We enjoy God, and it is a delight to ourselves! When we so pursue God, he will make us to ride on the high hills of the earth! He will feed us with the heritage of Jacob, a spiritual feast of fatness! These promises are directly connected with observing the day the Lord gives in the manner appointed by the Lord. Is it any wonder that the church of today is so often weak and frail, when so often the Sabbath is dedicated to our pleasure alone, rather than taking pleasure in God? Do we go away from our Lord's days unfulfilled? Might it be because we have not come in the right way and for the right reasons?

Think also of the relative powerlessness of the church, and our apparent ineffectiveness in terms of impacting the communities in which we live. Observe the note of triumph which sounds for the people of God who delight themselves in God and in his day. He will cause them to ride on the high hills of the earth. Might it not be that a church more committed to the pursuit of God in the way God has mandated and on the day that God has mandated would see more success in extending the kingdom of her beloved Lord and Saviour, Jesus Christ? The Sabbath day is a testimonial day. Our sanctifying of it is a testimony of our being set apart to

God. The observance of God's day is a badge that the Christian wears before the world of allegiance to our Lord and Master, Jesus Christ. It is the day for spiritual nourishment, in which, by walking closely with God, drinking deeply of the fountain of living water, we come forth refreshed and reinvigorated. Our faith is revived and our hopes renewed for our battle with a world that hates us as it hated Christ. To fail to attend upon and enter into the spiritual exercises of the day, and simultaneously to fail to take oneself off from pursuing one's own pleasures, is like a soldier knowing that there is a battle looming, who absents himself from the drill exercises of his regiment, walks past the armoury, and spends the day gorging himself on food and drink.

The blessings outlined by Isaiah are types or shadows of spiritual prosperity. Spiritual prosperity is the great pursuit of the right-thinking Christian. Such a believer earnestly desires that he might be transformed by the renewing of his mind. Just think for a moment how much more holy and happy we might be if we truly and entirely gave ourselves more to the God-ordained means of sanctification, such as reading, prayer, and the worship of God. It is when we behold the glory of the Lord that we are transformed into the same image, from glory to glory (2 Corinthians 3:18). For what greater blessing, or for what higher motivation and purpose, and what greater peace and joy, could we ever ask or seek? This is the foretaste of glory, when the earthy man that we are shall take on completely the character of the spiritual man.

Sabbath songs

Consider Psalm 92, the "Song for the Sabbath day." Here you find a great confluence of these themes and aims, like streams flowing into a great river. We might almost construct a theology of Lord's day worship, activity, and thought around the words of this psalm. See how it opens with a burst of praise to God, which delights the soul of the psalmist. It is good, in every sense of the word, to give thanks to the Lord! Observe how the writer has been made glad through the work of God, how he triumphs in the work of God's hands. He magnifies God, decrying the ignorance and folly (moral blindness) of the God-denier. He compares the everlasting destruction of the wicked with the everlasting exaltedness of God, before whom all enemies shall be scattered (*cf* Numbers 10:35). But the psalmist himself, the God-worshipper, finds his strength, joy, blessing, and salvation in God. He flourishes, he is richly blessed: another image of prosperity and fulfilment. How glorious is the character of a true believer, and how wonderful his spiritual prosperity (v14-15)!

> Those who are planted in the house of the Lord
>> Shall flourish in the courts of our God.
>> They shall still bear fruit in old age;
>> They shall be fresh and flourishing,
>> To declare that the Lord is upright;
>> He is my rock, and there is no unrighteousness in him.

If we would have this be our character, ought we not to be planted in the house of the Lord? If we are not flourishing spiritually, might it be because we are not entering into the courts of our God with the right intent, and entering into the purposes of the day with all our heart and mind and soul and strength? There can be few greater blessings than these, promised to the saints of God for such simple acts of obedience. Here are the people: "those who are planted." Here is the place: "in the house of the Lord," "in the courts of our God." Here is the promise: "they shall still bear fruit in old age, they shall be fresh and flourishing." What a simple, secure, and certain recipe for long-term usefulness and fruitfulness and happiness! Why, then, would anyone dream of cutting themselves off from the least of the services of the house of God? Why would any deprive themselves of such by poor preparation and practice of these principles, or a pale pursuit of these purposes?

We speak of blessing and pleasure. For what more could we ask than to know that God the righteous is our Rock, and to be fresh and flourishing in him, fruitful into old age? Is it any great cost to turn away from our own pleasures, from our own ways and words, and to delight ourselves in the Lord, when in doing so we glorify and enjoy him in such exquisite pleasures?

Let the world mock! Let the world tell us that it wants no part of our pleasures! Still less do we want any part of theirs. "The natural man does not receive the things of the Spirit of God, for they are foolishness to him; nor can he know them, because they are spiritually discerned" (1 Corinthians 2:14). These are things of which the world knows nothing truly. The world does not know the source from which these pleasures flow, and therefore it does not know the pleasures which flow from the source. They know neither the fountain, nor the sweet streams which pour from it.

The worldling's pleasures are fading; all this fallen world's "boasted pomp and show" will be seen to be empty. This world will be judged, and will pass away, and its pleasures will pass with it. Christ's kingdom is not of this world (John 18:36), and the joys and delights and blessings of Christ's kingdom are not of this world. These are solid joys and lasting treasures, which none but Zion's children know.

But how will we achieve these purposes? What should we actually do on the Lord's day? How should we behave? The purpose and practice of the Lord's day are closely linked. The purpose bounds and is furthered by the practice, and the practice is informed by and pursues the purpose.

3
THE PRACTICE OF THE LORD'S DAY

So far we have constructed a great steam engine out of the principle of the Lord's day. We have stoked its engine with the coals of purpose, and built up a head of steam. However, if this vehicle is to travel in a God-honouring fashion, it must do so along the four biblical rails of practice, which must be greased with the oils of planning and preparation.

In laying these tracks on which the Lord's day train is to run, we must remember that it is neither possible nor remotely productive to set out to provide an exhaustive list of 'dos and don'ts' for the right use of the Lord's day. Evidently, that risks falling into the habit of the Pharisees. They actually made a mockery of the true purpose of the Sabbath by an obsessive and legalistic approach. However, it is a very easy habit to fall into, and for what may appear to be the best of reasons. Many of us will have a tendency, when we hear the principles, to ask "Well, what about... ?" We immediately bring particular situations, rather than general examples, into the equation. We often try to get the principle applied for that and all other similar situations. We attempt to create a universal rule, or at least a universal application of the rule. In effect, we might want a list of regulations that tells us, "Under circumstances A, B or C, the only way to be righteous is to do X."

However, we need to recognise that, while some instances are black and white (and what we are saying now is no excuse for fudging those issues), much of this is a matter of an instructed conscience. These principles must be rigorously and righteously applied using 'sanctified common-sense.' The desire for a set of rules is often (though not always) an indicator of spiritual immaturity or spiritual laziness. More legitimately, it might be a young Christian who has never been this way before, or someone seeking to apply these things for the first time. There are indications even in the course of revelation that this is a matter in which Christ shows much patience in making the truth clear. Less legitimately, the problem might be an older believer who has never sought to exercise spiritual discernment. It could even be simply that we would rather have someone else do our thinking for us.

Other men's consciences cannot be the final arbiters. "He, whose institution alone it is, has a right to prescribe how it shall be kept. Remember to keep it holy."[1] The word of God is the rule of faith and life, not the opinion of other men, however much other men might help us to discern the true application of God's word. There is certainly space to take counsel. Pastors, friends, parents, and others, might be able to provide advice on particular issues. Brothers and sisters might wish to use trusted friends as 'quality control.' We might ask a particular person to undertake to nudge our conscience into action if we are seen doing something which brings a question to their mind about its propriety on the Lord's day. The verdict of an instructed conscience might then be, "I believe this falls within the scope of what God's Word permits," or, "I conclude this falls within the scope of what the Lord forbids."

We need to help each other in these regards, and there are times and places for appropriate discussion. As local churches, our great aim ought to be the glory of God. We ought to look out for one another, and help each other to make informed decisions. As brothers, we ought to be concerned for one another.

Guidelines and warnings

All that said, it is good to be clear on the things that are clear. It is also helpful to make certain guidelines for ourselves on the basis of these principles. If we do so, we need to make sure of two things.

Firstly, that by doing so we do not make an opportunity for Satan. Without the law there is no knowledge of sin. If we make our own laws then we will afflict our consciences unnecessarily, and make problems for ourselves and others, the existence of which God never intended.

Secondly, there is a risk that by setting up a rule for ourselves we will then set ourselves up as the judges of others in a wrong way. There is a great tendency, when we establish a standard for ourselves, that we immediately make it, even unconsciously, the mark by which we assess all others. So, for example, one might say, "I believe it would be sin in me to go for a bike ride on the Lord's day." He does so because he cycles to work every day, or goes out to exercise on his bike every evening, and he has decided that it would be best to take a break from his cycling on the Lord's day.[2] A few days later his friend cycles past on Sunday afternoon. What is his response? Perhaps some might say, "I never knew so-and-so was so degenerate!" But what if that friend is cycling peacefully to clear his head in anticipation of the Lord's day evening meeting? What if he is on his way to meet someone else for Bible study? What if he is on his way to church by bike? There is space here for the exercise of genuine Christian liberty. Counsel may be sought, and is available, and guidelines may be set, but the spirit of legalism is alive and well. That spirit is to be guarded against at all costs. The way to ensure this is to set our standard according to God's standard, and neither to lower our own below the Lord's, nor seek to raise it above.

A further word concerning liberty: there is an opposite tendency, and one that is equally rife. Many of us, when we discern a standard, effectively ask the question, "How far can I go before I am actually sinning?" This is then painted as an exercise in Christian liberty. It is not. It is flirting with sin, cultivating license. Our question ought to be, "What can I do, and how can I do it, most to honour God, and put myself safely and squarely within the scope of his revealed will?" We need to discern not, negatively, everything that is permissible before we fall into sin, but, positively, everything we can do in order to honour God with all that we have and are.

We need a true Christian spirit. We must cultivate a heart that pursues obedience but recognises a brother of weaker conscience. We need to be sensitive to character, maturity, and tendency, but fierce in our underlying obedience to the Lord.

The Bible itself does not give us an exhaustive list of precepts covering every eventuality, but it does set down four very clear principles of practice for the Lord's day. If we focus upon the purpose of the Lord's day, seeking to act by the practical principles provided, we shall find that many objections, cavils, and apparent difficulties melt away.

However, before we look at the actual practice of the Lord's day—the four rails on which we run—it is valuable to consider how we might grease those rails by our planning and preparation for the Lord's day. It is an axiom in many fields that 'to fail to prepare is to prepare to fail.' The same might be said of the Lord's day. When our Lord instructed us, "Do not worry about tomorrow, for tomorrow will worry about its own things; sufficient for the day is its own trouble" (Matthew 6:34), he was not advocating irresponsibility, poor stewardship, or carelessness. Too often, this is the approach of the people of God to the Lord's day.

Planning and preparation

Imagine (or remember!) what it is like to love the most wonderful person in the world, but not to be able to see them every day. Perhaps you have been in one of those long distance relationships where you can have some kind of occasional contact. Nevertheless, opportunities actually to spend time in each other's company are rare, perhaps only once every few months, or once a month, or even once a week. This wonderful day approaches, when you shall actually see and spend time with your beloved. What eagerness! What preparation! What longing! What intent and planning to ensure that not one minute of that precious time is wasted! Diaries are emptied. Other demands, even legitimate ones, are put aside. For days, perhaps even weeks, all scheduling and planning is worked out with this day in mind. Finally, all is made ready in quivering anticipation. You may think that I have overcooked this illustration a little, but you know what I mean!

Is this not at least something of the attitude and anticipation with which we should approach the day which the Lord our God has appointed for meeting with his people? What did you do last Saturday night? How did you feel when you woke up on Sunday morning?

What preparations have we made, as individuals, as families, and as churches, immediately (and further) in advance of the Lord's day, to put in and get out the most from the day set apart to the Lord our God?

There is a potential danger in all this. We need to make sure that we aim at consistent holiness throughout the week, not merely a high but hypocritical display on and around the Lord's day. Christianity is a 24/7 religion. The world is full of nominal Christians whose Sunday performances are simply an effective act before men. Those impressive appearances are belied by the shabby and shallow—or downright contradictory—behaviour of the other six days. The best preparation for the Lord's day will be the persistent pursuit of a distinctive and consistent walk before God throughout all the week. At the same time, the world has its fair share of Christians who believe that, because 'all of life is worship,' that they do not need to look at the Lord's day as any different from any other day. However, there are things we can do and ought to do on the Lord's day. We should do all we can to make the most of the day on which we particularly look and long for deeper communion with God. Many of these points ought to be true during the week, but the special presence of God on the Lord's day demands particular care in certain respects.

The outward man

There are many ways in which we can and ought to

prepare ourselves for the Lord's day, even in very practical ways—taking care of the outward man. For example, for many of us, Saturdays might be days of household duties, or other chores and responsibilities. Others have full normal working days. Are we seeking to ensure that, come Saturday night, we are making an effort to be in bed in good time and well rested in preparation for the Sunday to follow? For many, Saturday night, like Friday, is a night for going out and staying out late. What manner of preparation is this for the Lord's day? If anything, for families, Saturday night ought to be at least as sacrosanct as a 'school night.' For some, it might be as basic as avoiding certain foods on Saturday night that leave us feeling dopey and slow on Sunday mornings. For others, it might require more complex thought and planning.

Sunday is also, for many, a day on which a substantial meal is to be cooked and eaten at lunchtime. (Incidentally, it is worth making sure that our 'Sunday lunch' does not become an occasion of heavy indulgence which actually stops us using the day for the best purposes.) In some homes, early Saturday evening therefore becomes a time of corporate family activity. I know homes in which meat is prepared, vegetables peeled and chopped and left in water overnight, desserts and puddings made. Much can be accomplished to minimise the amount of work that needs to be done on the Lord's day. The whole family can be mobilised (perhaps, it must be said, with varying degrees of willingness!) to accomplish all the work that needed to be done. The tidying and cleaning has to be done. Clothes can be prepared in order to avoid the panicked and distracting pursuit of something reasonably clean and vaguely presentable on the Lord's day morning. There may be other practical efforts that need to be made on Saturday afternoon and evening, or even earlier, in order to be prepared for the Lord's day. It may be as simple as buying food and filling the car with petrol before the end of the week. It is a simple matter of thinking ahead.

This also has ramifications for Sunday morning. For how many (perhaps leading on from those late Saturday nights) are Sunday mornings for late rising followed by frantic activity, in order to be at the services in good time? Of course, emergencies and surprises will arise (especially in families). Nevertheless, the ordering of our time and efforts on Sunday mornings ought to be with the aim of a full and unobstructed appreciation of the whole day. This might even come down to ensuring that adequate time is left for the journey to church without breaking the speed limit, or getting stuck behind some slowcoach, doing nothing for our spiritual equilibrium. Too often, individuals, couples or families can arrive at church trying to give the impression of spiritual joy and light, while inside there is only seething frustration and barely-contained irritability. We mask it by the cheesy greeting, of course, but it is there, and it hardly helps us be ready to seek the face of God.

The inward man

That is why we ought also to prepare the inward man. In saying that, we are not trying to set up a false distinction between the outward and the inward. We need to recognise that these will flow into and out of each other. Even as we seek to ensure that in terms of our physical preparation we are ready for Sunday, so we need to prepare mentally, emotionally, and spiritually.

In what frame of mind and heart do you arrive at the services on the Lord's day? Particular preparation to remove all obstacles to the glorifying and enjoyment of God on the Lord's day should again begin on Saturday. What do you do on Saturday afternoon, and particularly in the evening? What films or television programmes do you watch on Saturday nights? How do you fill your last waking hours or minutes before the Lord's day, and the first of them on the Lord's day? Is it with matter that will enable you to wake, or promote your waking, in the fittest possible spiritual state to worship God?

In Richard Baxter's Kidderminster, the young people used to gather together on Saturday evenings to praise God and pray together. Baxter makes the point that this provides for the spiritual coals simply to be raked over, rather than a new fire lit on Sunday morning. The former is much easier to do than the latter. Do Sunday evening family devotions make the coming Lord's day a particular concern, in terms of focused preparation of the heart, and prayer poured out to God? What about family relationships? Are there are any matters that have arisen during the course of the week that need to be dealt with? What about others with whom you will gather in worship on the Lord's day? Our Lord commands that,

> if you bring your gift to the altar, and there remember that your brother has something against you, leave your gift there before the altar, and go your way. First be reconciled to your brother, and then come and offer your gift.
>
> — MATTHEW 5:23-24

We ought to be able to gather as a church at peace with one another. To do otherwise makes a mockery of worship. To come into God's presence with our brothers to worship him as the united body of Christ, when we are not truly united in heart, is to invite Satan to come into the congregation with us. Unresolved tensions or disputes between husbands and wives, parents and children, or church members, can be like Achan's wedge of gold in Israel (the story can be found in Joshua 7). It can effectively rob not only the individuals involved but the church as a whole of the felt presence and real power of God. We therefore need to ensure that there are no outstanding issues between ourselves that need to be resolved.

Thinking it through

This may sound contradictory, but it may be that there are matters (outward or inward) that need to be dealt with as a matter of urgency to prevent them becoming a distraction on the Lord's day. These, perhaps, ought to be completed, or somehow dealt with. Undone 'homework'—of child or adult—may be a cause of agitation throughout the day if it is not properly dealt with in advance so that it can legitimately be set aside. Sometimes we need to work harder or earlier or later on the other six days in order to be free from distraction on the Lord's day. We need to clear the decks for holy action.

Sunday mornings, again, are important. The outward preparation ought to be with a view to providing for spiritual readiness. An early night on Saturday provides for the raking over on the Lord's day morning of the coals that were set alight on the previous evening, as private and family worship sets the tone for the day. Preparation of food, clothing, and other such matters, ensures that the Lord's day is as free as possible from unnecessary encumbrances. The minimising of disruptive influences, and of those things which might introduce disruptive influences, provides for a far greater likelihood of a better state of mind and heart when we arrive at worship.

Again, we cannot guarantee perfect and seamless preparation that will not be disturbed. Neither can we guarantee that the preparation will be entirely effective.

We have an enemy who is, so far as God allows him, seeking to orchestrate events so as to wreck not just the Lord's day, but every part of our walk with God. One older writer characterises Satan as standing at our side as we seek to write a perfect script, jogging our elbow. That does not mean that we stop writing. It means that we have to take account of the fact that there will be efforts made to undermine our attempts at holiness. We need, therefore, to arm ourselves for the battle. We must prepare as adequately as we are able, in dependence upon the Spirit of God and in obedience to the Lord's revealed will.

Light from the past

Let us turn our attention now to consider how the prepared man or woman of God sets out to employ the hours of the Christian Sabbath for the purpose for which they were intended. These four rails on which the train runs are framed below in the language of one of the classical catechisms of Reformed Christianity, the *Westminster Shorter Catechism*, and its Baptist sister-documents. It could be argued that, in doing so, we will simply be perpetuating a merely Puritan view of the Lord's day, rather than embracing a truly biblical approach. Let me briefly address such concerns.

First, we have so far been considering the biblical validity of the principle and purpose of the Lord's day. I trust that the biblical validity of its practice will also be evident as we work through it. In other words, though the phrasing is drawn from the Catechism, the substance is drawn from the Scriptures.

Second, I do think we must take care when adopting Puritan language and inheriting biblical convictions filtered through the grid of Puritanism. We must recognise the peculiar circumstances and challenges of Puritanism.[3] The Puritan view of the Sabbath was forged, in part, out of the crucible of the battle over the Lord's day. As part of this combat, King James I and King Charles I were issuing their "Book of Sports" in defence of certain 'recreations' on the Lord's day. They were deliberately contending against the Puritan view of the Lord's day. That Book of Sports was issued first by James I in 1618, in response to what his son Charles I later described (in his 1633 "Declaration of Sports") as King James' horror at finding his Lancastrian subjects "debarred from lawful recreations upon Sundays after evening prayers ended, and upon Holy-days." In other words, he was horrified by the rising embrace (or, perhaps, enforcement) of the Puritan view.

We must note that the battle was not, first and foremost, over whether or not there was a Lord's day. Again, I am painting here with a fairly broad historical brush. It was generally recognised in what was sometimes called Christendom (if you will permit the label) that the first day of the week was a special holy day. That was true even if the grounds of that recognition were not always well-developed, or were merely formal. What the Puritans were contending for was the right use of that day against the abuses current in a society so heavily influenced by forces different to those which affect us.

The Puritan Sabbath which has been bequeathed to us through the Confessions and Catechisms and other such documents was a theology of the Lord's day which had been developed over time. For example, the proto-Puritan William Perkins (1558-1602) in his *Golden Chain* provides a recognisably 'Puritan' approach to recreation on the Lord's day. That approach came to its full-orbed expression in contention against deliberately opposing views. These convictions were not simply the product of the Puritans' eventual and only-relative legislative supremacy. Nevertheless, they were forged in an environment in which there was something of a cultural consensus that the first day of the week was at least in some respects a day having to do with God. That meant different things to different people. However, in that context, assumptions were usually made about the very foundation of society as a Christian one, even if that was a substantially nominal notion.

The environment in which the Lord's day (working out the Sabbath principle) was inherited and observed by the early church was different. The early believers had no cultural or legislative supremacy. Often they had little or no stake in the culture. They were granted no legislative or sometimes even public voice. They lived in a profoundly pagan environment. All manner of religious observances proliferated and their own religious convictions were often either dismissed or quashed, if not deliberately assaulted. The whole tenor of society was as different from the Puritan period as the Puritan period is from ours. How many converted Roman slaves could assume that they would obtain leave for Christian worship on the first day of the week? How many converted Jews working within a Judaistic structure of time found it difficult to devote the first rather than the seventh day to the Lord?[4] What patterns and rhythms of life informed their application of the principles and purposes of the Lord's day? What does this have to say to believers today who live in cultures where there is no presumption about the first day of the week as a day of rest (however formal or abused such a notion might be)?

At the same time, we are far from the first to wrestle with these things. The great Baptist pastor-theologian, Andrew Fuller, wrote a letter to a friend who was struggling with this. It seems that the friend was tying himself in knots, and Fuller was trying to cut them. The pastor tried to condense his reasoning into a short space:

> If the keeping of a sabbath to God were not in all ages binding, why is it introduced in the moral law, and founded upon God's resting from his works? If it were merely a Jewish ceremonial, why do we read of time being divided by weeks before the law? There was a day in the time of John the apostle which the Lord called his own; and as you do not suppose this to be the seventh, (for, if it were, we ought still to keep it,) you must allow it to be the first. The first day then ought to be kept as the Lord's own day, and we ought

not to think our own thoughts, converse on our own affairs, nor follow our own business on it. To say, as you do, that we must not eat our own supper on that day is requiring what never was required on the Jewish sabbath. Necessary things were always allowed. Nor did my argument from 1 Cor. xi. suppose this. The argument was—the ordinance of breaking bread being called the Lord's supper proved that they ought not to eat their own supper while eating that supper; therefore the first day being called the Lord's day proves we ought not to follow our own unnecessary concerns while that continues, but to devote it to the Lord, and this is a moral duty—that, whatever day we keep, we keep it to the Lord.[5]

We must recognise that we might readily inherit the biblical principles, purposes and practices which the Puritans and others have enshrined in their own language. We would be fools to ignore the considered assessment of men like Sutcliff, well read in church history, who concluded,

one thing, all who are conversant with the pages of ecclesiastical history must allow, that when, either in general or particular instances, any eminent measures of the life and power of religion have been discovered, a proportionable regard for the sanctification of the Lord's day, has been manifested.[6]

Wise applications

We must labour to make sure our own applications are wise and thoughtful. For example, the so-called 'Judaeo-Christian heritage' that has informed so much of the development of the modern West is being eroded. You may have your own convictions about such a process. However, we must recognise that, for example, a believer's right to abstain from unnecessary labour on the Lord's day is increasingly being threatened. The culture is shifting again, and our application of the principles and practices is going to be informed by such a shift. That is not to say that it will necessarily become easier or harder. Rather, we cannot blindly assume that the particular and distinctive battles of the Puritans are precisely the same as ours at the point of application. We must therefore prayerfully and carefully labour to apply the biblical truth to our own circumstances.

In saying all this, I am not seeking to give us an easy way to shrug off our holy and healthy privileges and obligations. We cannot simply say, when we come up against something difficult or costly, "Well, that would have been fine for a Puritan, but it's not possible today!" Rather, it is again to demand that we do not fall, perhaps with the best of intentions, into a lazy or legalistic approach to application.

This section will be fairly short. Do you wonder why this one negative and these three positive rails can be dealt with so briefly? It is, in essence, because they are so simple and, at root, biblical. They are so closely bound up with the principle and purpose of the Lord's day that to extend them would be largely to reiterate or simply repeat what we have already considered. In themselves, the principles are clear and brief, but the applications are almost endless. Consider and rejoice in our gospel liberty! Here we have entered into the freedom of adults, rather than the restrictions applied to the young. Consider also what a blessing this is compared to the impositions of Pharisaism. Here are four rails, clean and broad and enabling us to travel forward, rather than the 1521 prohibitions of legalistic Judaism, all throwing a brake on our joy in God in Christ.

REST FROM OUR ORDINARY EMPLOYMENT AND RECREATION

(Exodus 20:10; Isaiah 58:13; Nehemiah 13:22)

The Lord's day is a day on which we consciously put aside those things which are legitimate on the other six days of the week. We follow our Creator, who rested on this day from the work of creation. God himself ceased from his regular employment on the preceding six days. Exodus 20:10 tells us that we are to do no work on that day—the idea is of customary activity, the things that we usually do. Indeed, "what may be lawful, what may be duty on another day, may be, and in numerous instances is, absolutely sinful on this. Make conscience of your conduct."[7]

Consider again the words of God through Isaiah. He warns us to turn our feet away from doing our own pleasure on the Lord's day. It is not a day on which we indulge ourselves in those worldly pleasures for which we do not have time on the other six days. Our own ways, pleasure, and words are put aside. Nehemiah pointed out the sin of doing business that did not need to be done on the Sabbath. Note also that Exodus 20 implies the sinfulness of creating unnecessary work for others. In other words, we should actively pursue giving all men their sabbath rest, whether they think they want it or not. For example, the fact that someone is already working in a store or restaurant on the Lord's day is no excuse for us to go shopping for non-emergency supplies on that day, or 'eating out' if there is no necessity. The sabbath principle requires that we make provision so that others "may rest as well as you" (Deuteronomy 5:14).

Most regular, normal activities can be and are to be simply and sweepingly set aside on the Lord's day. Observe that this putting aside is a conscientious effort involving the whole of our humanity. There are some who find it hard to take a holiday. They chafe at the bit until they are back in harness. It can be the same on the Lord's day. Our rest from our ordinary employments can be forced and unwilling. Our body may be away from the workplace, but our minds and hearts are not. How hard it can be to set aside the pursuits of the other six days! How often, for example, do children see or hear their friends out playing in the streets or fields? Often they may even be directly invited to participate. "Can so-and-so come out to play?" is a refrain that can cause immense grief if it is carelessly employed on the Lord's day. This is not because fun and joy are somehow outlawed on Sundays, or because all forms of recreation become out-of-bounds. It is because the pursuit of joy takes another and better form.

Screens and sports

It can get even more difficult in the age of the smartphone. If kids no longer go out to play, they certainly have endless diversions at their fingertips. Sometimes the adults have more. Social media applications, with a constant stream of demands and alerts, sports events and scores, with a constant stream of updates and alerts, the electronic marketplace, with its constant stream of opportunities and alerts. I imagine that many if not most of my readers—and I certainly include myself—have faced this battle with demanding distraction, sometimes in the very worship of God.

There are pleasures that in themselves would be legitimate on any other day of the week, but they may be arranged for a Sunday. We know that they are taking place, we know when they are taking place. There may be a yearning after them that threatens to take our minds off the higher and purer pleasures and blessings of the Lord's day. Think of the ache in the schoolboy's heart as he draws near to the school gate on a day when the sun is shining and all creation beckons him to walk on by and spend the day in happy wanderings. That can be replicated in the Christian who knows that he must give up something of which he is enamoured, or even to which he is merely attracted, 'simply' because it takes place on the Lord's day Sabbath. And yet there are times when it must be so.

Perhaps the modern idols of sport and entertainment are among the most prominent battlegrounds. The old preacher, David Clarkson, lamented that "many had rather spend that time which the Lord has allotted for their souls, in sports and recreations, than in the public worship; think one whole day in seven too much, will rob God of all, or part of it, to recreate themselves."[8] Whether it is watching or participating, ourselves or with family members, the modern sports arena is a temple which too readily rivals the household of God. We may not be trying to arrange our Sunday worship around some big sporting event, or worse still, weaving the sporting event into our Sunday worship. Even so, the rarely-subtle and often-throttling pressure of Sunday practice or Sunday matches mean that we persuade ourselves that we, or more likely our children, need to invest to sport in a way that trumps the Lord's day. We allow that pressure to chip away at our alleged commitment to being in God's presence with God's people on God's day. We explain why this time, for this season, under these circumstances, just for a while, it must be so. The same can happen with other entertainments. It is amazing how often people who can arrange a whole week around a particular interest cannot arrange a single day or even hour around the God whom they claim to worship.

Deliberate rest

This 'putting aside' must be a matter of the mind and heart as well as the body. We need to school our thinking and feeling, as well as our doing, so that we are free from the things which legitimately take up our time and attention on the other six days, but which too readily intrude into the Lord's day.

This does not make Sunday a day of inactivity. It means that we avoid concentrating on the things that normally take up our time and attention—what we read, listen to, think about, watch, or do. God was still engaged in sustaining and guiding his created world on the seventh day. In the words of John Sutcliff,

> The first idea of a sabbath seems then to be, "a laying aside of our usual business." Agreeably to this, we find it expressly enjoined in the fourth commandment, "in it thou shalt do no manner of work." But are we to stop here? Are we to consider it merely as a day of inactivity and indolence? If so, the most slothful would bid fair to keep it best.--No;--let us not so disparage this sacred day. The interruption of our worldly business, is in order that we may have leisure for, attention to, and activity in, what is proper to the day.[9]

It is not, then, a day of inactivity. Rather, ceasing from our customary activities frees the day for holy activity. It becomes a day for the energetic pursuit of God.

ACTS OF PIETY

(Exodus 20:8; Deuteronomy 5:12; Isaiah 58:13-14; Luke 4:16; Acts 20:7; 1 Corinthians 16:2; Revelation 7:9*ff*)

The great focus of our time and energy on the Lord's day should be worship—private, family, and public worship. We are to "keep it holy" (Exodus 20:8), taking all pains to use it for the purposes for which God intended it. This is an active aim, and it means a definite seeking after God. It does not mean that we drift along and seek to catch the spirit of others. It means that each one of us sets out to engage with prepared heart, mind, and soul, in the various acts of worship which make up the day. Spurgeon asks,

> Is it not a heavenly joy to sit still on the one day of rest, and to be fed with the finest of the wheat? I have known men made capable of bearing great trials--personal, relative, pecuniary, and the like--because they have looked backward upon one Sabbatic feast, and then forward to another. They have said in their hour of trouble,—"Patience, my heart; the Lord's day is coming, when I shall drink and forget my misery. I

shall go and sit with God's people, and I shall have fellowship with the Father and with the Son, and my soul shall be satisfied as with marrow and fatness, till I praise the Lord with joyful lips."[10]

Public worship was clearly one of the key appointments of the new covenant church on the Lord's day, and we should not forsake the assembling of ourselves together (Hebrews 10:24-25). We must take pains to enter in with eager expectation. "When we are weary of a thing, take no pleasure in it, we easily give way to any suggestion that may disparage it. Let the worship of God be your delight, the joy and solace of your souls."[11] Our public worship should exemplify the activity of our day, not be the exception to it. In private, and in our families, we are to pursue that spirit and activity of worship here on earth, which we anticipate as our privilege and duty above (Revelation 7:9ff.). It is, above all else, a day for celebrating our blessings in Christ. It is a weekly season for exercising our blood-bought liberty in the worship of God, dwelling upon who God is and all that he has done. Indeed, "the *degree* of that relish you have for the *Sabbath*, may be considered as a *rule* by which you may measure the *state* of religion in your souls."[12]

With this in mind, and with a view to honouring God and obtaining his mercies, we ought to be biblically inventive and proactive. I say 'biblically' because all our worship must not transgress the directives that God has laid down for his worship. This approach is commonly called 'the regulative principle'—the idea that worship is to consist only of those things which God has specifically prescribed. I say 'inventive and proactive' because, within those God-ordained limits, we ought to exercise ourselves to maximise our pursuit of God. Are we doing everything we could and should be doing? Are there patterns in our private lives which we could alter in a closer pursuit of this ideal? Are there elements of our public worship which we could alter in order to bring the biblical purpose of the Lord's day to the fore? Are there activities in which we could engage as the people of God which would foster our aims on the Lord's day? Many Christians find it far easier to provide a list of things that we cannot do than of things we can and should do.

The pursuit of God

This pursuit of God does not begin when we arrive at the church building for a morning service of worship. It does not end when we leave any afternoon meetings, or the evening service at the end of the day. It is not restricted to our public gatherings, although it reaches a particular height in them. Some prefer to begin taking account of it at sundown on Saturday, according to a more Jewish pattern, which means it 'ends' at sundown on Sunday. I do not think that is necessary (though preparations, as we have seen, are useful). It usually begins when we wake in the morning, but not in an artificial or mechanical way. We do not set a timer or stopwatch, as if trying to make sure we mark off the minutes, or at least accomplish the bare minimum. Besides, what would that mean for sundown on Sunday, if observed in that way? Would that prove the starting pistol for some kind of post-sabbath party? Not at all! Such questions would betray the wrong approach entirely! This is our day of worship, and everything we do ought to revolve around that. Worship is to be our priority, our privilege, and our delight on the Lord's day. We get to make the most of it!

Of course, we need to recognise the particular difficulties for some. Sisters in Christ with unconverted husbands, or husbands with unbelieving wives, may face particular trials. The church ought to support and encourage such spiritual family members through those difficulties as they seek to honour God without sinfully rejecting the dynamics of the home, whether it be the headship of the husband or any other relationship.[13] Christian children in the homes of unbelieving or unsympathetic parents face a similar struggle, especially when they are younger. Yes, they are to obey God rather than men, but they need also to maintain, as far as they are able, an honest and manifested respect for the parental authority which Christ has instituted over them. There can be phenomenal pressure in some families to make Sunday a 'family day' at the expense of a wholehearted pursuit of Christian duty and delight. Too many believers forget that they have become part of a family which calls for a greater commitment. Christian parents with unbelieving and unwilling children are also likely to face problems, particularly as the children grow older. The parents' appreciation of their own God-given authority in the family realm must be well-grounded if they are to ride out the storm.

Whether in private or public, it ought to be a day for the seeking of God. We ought to maximise our investments. Far too many of us are seeking to give God a nod, before demanding the rest of the day for ourselves. For example, the language of 'morning worship', with the assumption that this means we also have the opportunity for afternoon or evening worship, has become empty or even oppressive to many modern Christians. The vast majority of treatments of worship today typically make casual or deliberate reference to a single opportunity for worship. That is not necessarily wrong, but is it best? Could we give more and get more?

However, we should bear in mind that this principle also allows for us to take account of other opportunities for the glory of God.

ACTS OF MERCY

(Matthew 12:9-14 *cf* Luke 14:1-6; Luke 13:15-17; 1 Corinthians 16:2)

Ceasing from our customary work, and actively engaging in worship, does not issue in cruelty to others. The Lord Christ healed a man with a withered hand, and used the example of caring for an ox or donkey, or rescuing it from a ditch, to illustrate the lawfulness of doing good on the Sabbath.

Members of the emergency services, the military, and medical personnel, for example, need not worry on account of their work if it demands their attentions on the Lord's day. It should be said, though, that they might still actively pursue, whenever and to whatever extent possible, their full engagement with the people of God.

It is not wrong to do good on the Lord's day. Some acts of mercy are incidental and occasional, such as responses to emergencies. There may also be, and should be, acts of mercy that Christians can or must actively pursue on the Lord's day, such as visiting and caring for and feeding others, so long as these things do not thoughtlessly override the first two practical principles. This is vital to take into account, for many unbelievers and some believers assume that a Christian who takes these things seriously has a mechanically legalistic approach to the matter. As Spurgeon says,

> Our Lord performed many of his noblest cures on the Sabbath, as if to show that the day was ordained to glorify God by yielding benefit to man. If at one time more than another the healing virtue flows freely from our Lord, it is on that one day in seven which is reserved for holy uses, and is called "the Lord's Day." Christ shows how suitable it is that a holy day should be crowned with holy deeds of mercy and love.[14]

That said, we must not use the 'mercy' line as an

excuse for doing what could have been done at some time during the week. Digging an elderly neighbour's garden, or washing his or her car, may be acts of mercy, but if unnecessarily carried out on the Lord's day then they may well contravene the first two principles. If you were driving home from church on a dark Sunday night and spotted someone with a burst tyre stranded alone by the side of the road, it would be an act of mercy to stop and assist that person. It would not necessarily be an act of mercy if you offered to help a neighbour swap his tyres in his driveway on the Lord's day. On the other hand, if it is a neighbour whose heavily pregnant wife needs to get to hospital pretty quickly, you ought to be the first to swing into action. Properly understood, the principle is relatively easily applied.[15]

ACTS OF NECESSITY

(Matthew 12:1-8; Luke 13:15-17)

The two great examples of acts of necessity recorded in Scripture are eating food and caring for animals. A family must provide food for itself, and a farmer must care for his animals. Milking cattle, for example, would be both necessity for the farmer and mercy for the cows. In our society, other tasks might be added. A skeleton crew is needed in some industries to keep society functioning, such as the power industry, or perhaps aspects of public transport. The military cannot stand down at weekends.

This is not a reason to keep an ordinary workload on an employee on this day, but gives room to do those things that cannot be left to another day. Again, this is not to be used as an excuse. It may be necessary and merciful to buy painkillers on Sunday if you have unexpectedly run out. It is not necessary to go food shopping because you did not plan that into your weekly schedule, or because a child is complaining that he or she wants a particular drink or packet of sweets. (Note that works of necessity and mercy can be difficult to separate or differentiate. That is not a problem, so long as the underlying point is clear.)

Doing homework is not a necessity, especially when it could and should have been completed during the week or on Saturday. Things put off until Sunday are not necessities. If we genuinely have too much 'homework' (and that applies to adults as much as it does to children) we need to look at our whole schedule and reconfigure it according to what ought to be our priorities.

Practical challenges

To give more detailed examples, a military officer, running a tight shift pattern, will be obliged to undertake certain duties on the Lord's day. These duties might be necessary to keep his unit or vessel running smoothly and functioning fully. He is aware of the issues, and can undertake his duties in good conscience. Are there, though, duties which can be completed by extra labour and preparation in the preceding days? Can he carry out those duties in advance and so enable him to keep his workload on the Lord's day to the bare minimum *i.e.* works of necessity alone? If so, he ought to seek to undertake those responsibilities in advance. The fact that there are some things that will have to be done on the Lord's day does not open up the day to doing anything that could be done. If there is opportunity to take time for reading and prayer, once his necessary duties are accomplished, he might then seek to undertake it, either alone or with others.

A businessman might need to be in a foreign city first thing Monday morning, but has some liberty to plan his own schedule. Could he make contact with a sister church, travel on the Saturday (if necessary seeking hospitality from the church that night), worship with the people of God on the Lord's day, and then go on to his place of business on Monday morning?

As the mother of a household plans for the Lord's day, does she need to leave the preparation of all the food and any tidying of the house for hospitality to Sunday morning? Or can she, even at the expense of other things, and with the help of her family, prepare as much as possible ahead of time so that the Lord's day is kept for only those things essential for the care of her family?

There are many industries where shift work is normal. This includes things like the pernicious 'four days on, four days off' schedule characteristic of staff at some modern airports, or similar patterns of work in the medical or transport field. Such shift work makes regular attendance at the services of the church difficult, if not impossible. In these circumstances, we should take into account the significance of what we are considering. We need to understand and appreciate the impact of principled obedience upon our brothers and sisters. With that in mind, might we not counsel them to consider finding employment where they can provide for themselves and their families while still honouring the Lord of the Sabbath? Might we not encourage them to consider swapping shifts, and assist them where possible? Could they make arrangements in the meantime so as to maximise their attendance at the church's gathering for worship and their own private devotions? Could we help their families where they themselves have few options? And would not this kind of consecration and sacrifice prove an eloquent lesson to those who regard Sunday football, or other sports, as more precious than the worship of God on the day he has appointed?

There are and will increasingly be real challenges in trying to run one's devotional life along these rails. It may not be long before the cultural and often merely formal structures that a nominal adherence to Christian religion has provided for Western society give way. These are structures within which the church in the West currently operates relatively freely and blessedly. But what if there is little or no employment that does not demand Sunday working? What if there are no protections for Christians persuaded of the validity of the Lord's day? What of those societies in which there are already no such structures and protections? What happens when the pattern of life (say, in an entirely agricultural community) places impositions on the structures of every day? What about societies that observe a different day of rest than the Christian day? The church does not respond by abandoning God's commands, but by pursuing them however it can. Again, this is not an excuse to indulge our own will, works and ways, and try to accommodate God around the fringes of our own appetites and activities.

A late sermon and the early church

Perhaps you know the story of sleepy Eutychus? Luke records it.

> Now on the first day of the week, when the disciples came together to break bread, Paul, ready to depart the next day, spoke to them and continued his message until midnight. There were many lamps in the upper room where they were gathered together. And in a window sat a certain young man named Eutychus, who was sinking into a deep sleep. He was overcome by sleep; and as Paul continued speaking, he fell down from the third story and was taken up dead. But Paul went down, fell on him, and

embracing him said, "Do not trouble yourselves, for his life is in him." Now when he had come up, had broken bread and eaten, and talked a long while, even till daybreak, he departed. And they brought the young man in alive, and they were not a little comforted.

— ACTS 20:7-12

This episode occurs in the midst of a blizzard of evangelistic and edifying activity carried out by Paul and a fairly large crew of companions. They arrive in Troas where Paul has an opportunity to instruct the saints. Reading some popular interpretations, one might imagine that Paul begins to preach at a fairly typical hour – perhaps six or seven o'clock, let us say. He finds himself a little carried away and gets his second wind at about 11pm. Still going strong at midnight, it all becomes a bit too much for Eutychus. Overcome with a mixture of boredom and weariness, he finally loses the battle against sleep and rolls out of his window seat to his doom, almost literally preached to death. But not to worry! The apostle simply heals him, and – undeterred – the callous preacher cracks on unrelentingly with his sermon until daybreak. Insensitive Paul! Inattentive Eutychus! The obvious lessons? Preachers should not go on too long and should make sure they maintain the attention of their hearers; or, hearers should care enough about the truth not to fall asleep while it is being preached.

But is that what is actually happening? I would suggest not.

You will notice, first of all, when they meet. It is on the first day of the week. As we have seen, this is that day on which the risen Christ made a repeated point of meeting with his disciples to speak truth to them for their blessing. Although the language of breaking bread does not require us to understand that this is a worship service in which the Lord's supper will be celebrated, it is not an unreasonable supposition.

On this occasion, these saints have the privilege of Paul himself being briefly present with them. The apostle takes the opportunity to explain the truth. It is clear that Paul preaches for some time, but it is also worth noting that we are not informed when he began preaching. That is important, because it might help us appreciate what is going on.

Could it be that what we have here is a congregation of believers from various backgrounds gathering as opportunity provides? Several sources inform us that Eutychus was a fairly common name for slaves. If this were the case here, then we might suggest that Eutychus, together with several others of the same or different circumstances, has made his way to worship once his day's work is done. Late at night or very early in the morning would be the only times when such meetings could occur for the whole church. It may even be feasible to suggest that Eutychus has already met with other saints at or before dawn.

For example, Pliny the Younger, governor and arch-complainer[16] of Bithynia-Pontus not many decades after these events, described Christians as being

> in the habit of meeting on a certain fixed day before it was light, when they sang in alternate verses a hymn to Christ, as to a god, and bound themselves by a solemn oath not to (do) any wicked deeds, never to commit any fraud, theft, or adultery, never to falsify their word, nor deny a trust when they should be called upon to deliver it up; after which it was their custom to separate, and then reassemble to partake of good food —but food of an ordinary and innocent kind.
>
> — BOOK TEN, LETTER 96

Without demanding this interpretation, I believe that the typical assumptions made of Paul and Eutychus are wrong. On the one hand, this is not Paul preaching a long and dull sermon without regard for the capacity of the hearers. On the other, this is not dopey Eutychus who simply cannot sustain his interest, or who is too young and weak to keep up the pace.

More likely is that we have here a group of committed and earnest believers who are seizing their opportunity to hear the Word of God from that fruitful servant of the Lord, Paul, before he moves on. They meet when they have their chance, perhaps at the very beginning or the end of the working day, or both. The one might have been earlier and the other later for the slaves, not to mention others in an environment where health and safety legislation would have tended toward the minimal. There were no restrictions on working hours for most of these people! The believers come, weary but eager, lighting the lamps in the room to enable them to make the most of the brief hours available. Yes, they are tired, preacher and hearers alike. Yes, it is warm. But this is a rich opportunity, and they are eager to make the most of it.

Far from criticising Paul for preaching too long or commiserating with Eutychus for being subjected to such an ordeal, we ought to be commending both men for their appetite for fellowship with God and his people. Yes, young Eutychus does eventually succumb to the atmosphere, and fall from the window. But notice that – once restored – it is not as if everyone decides to call it a night. They keep going until dawn breaks, and there is no indication that Paul locked the doors and put Sopater, Aristarchus, Secundus, Gaius, Timothy, Tychicus and Trophimus on the exits to prevent people leaving.

Leaving aside the legitimate practical question of engaging preachers and engaged listeners, I wonder how eager we are to meet with God and his people on the appointed day to hear the truth explained, proclaimed and applied? How determined are we to make the most of our opportunities for worship? Are we ready to swap shifts or make up hours in order to meet with the saints? If necessary, either because of persecution or some other necessity, would you be willing to meet before dawn and after dusk in order to worship the Lord your God in company with his people?

Eutychus sets us a good example. To be sure, rolling over in our beds is a lot safer than rolling over in an open window. However, taking into account all the issues, I think Eutychus was with the right people in the right place at the right time doing the right thing. Perhaps such questions are already a live issue for believers in Islamic countries, for example, or in those nations where there is no notion of a Christian influence or heritage. Again, these are the kinds of challenges which converted children in godless homes might have to take into account, or those with unconverted spouses.

How eager are you to be where God is making himself known through the preached word? Dawn and dusk meetings may again become a reality for those who set out to honour God's day within the confines of an unsympathetic or openly hostile society.

An appetite for God

These, then, are some of the thought processes and decisions that might and should characterise a believer seeking to honour the Lord's day. Obedience to God must be our priority, even at the expense of other legitimate labour and recreation. If necessary, heads of households might need to make those decisions and explain why, as a family, they will not and cannot take on those extra things, or must give up something that has been part of their schedule up to this point.

But is it so? What are we doing to promote the ends for which God has given the Sabbath to man? We cannot expect members of churches to pursue these things without instruction in them. We should not expect others to pursue these things without our seeking to be examples. In finishing this study, it might, then, be worth seeking to offer some practical thoughts and suggestions as to how we can best go about ordering the Lord's day to derive the blessings promised if we delight in God.

In any thoughts as to what would be appropriate activity for the Lord's day, we should go back to the purposes of the day. Does it contribute to the glory of God? Does it help me to enjoy communion with God? Am I likely to be blessed by God in it?

Am I really resting from my normal pursuits, works, and recreations? Am I actively engaging in (or contributing to my active engagement in) the worship of God by doing this? Is this a work of necessity, or should I have done it during the week? Could I leave it until tomorrow? Is this a genuine work of mercy?

We should be wary of adopting a Pharisaic, legalistic attitude to the Lord's day. This is not a day for the making of a thousand little rules and regulations that swamp our true aim and dampen all our holy enthusiasm. We need to avoid even the tendency to make Sunday a mere list of 'dos and don'ts', and be careful to judge ourselves in the light of God's word, and not to bind all others to the rules you may find it profitable to make for yourselves.

At the same time, we must consider the cost of carelessness with regard to the Lord's day. Sometimes Christians complain as if a high view of the Lord's day drives people away. Do we ever consider that a low view of the Lord's day might drive the Lord himself away? In Sutcliff's quaint language,

> May not a want of a proper regard to the sanctification of the Lord's-day, while it is an evidence of the low estate of religion with many, be considered as a cause why God stands at a distance from them, as to his reviving presence.[17]

If we desire the Lord to draw near to us, ought we not to be concerned about doing those things which please him? Might not a greater concentration on and investment in this day be one great means of glorifying God? The Lord has promised that he will honour those who honour him, but those who despise him shall be lightly esteemed (1 Samuel 2:30).

Practical suggestions

With these things in mind, the following suggestions are offered. They are not rules. They are intended to offer some channels down which the blessings of the Lord's day can run. Other channels can be dug; these can be widened or diverted. I am simply trying to give some hints as to the kind of areas which we can be thinking about.

Aim to attend all the public worship services of a faithful church, as long as you are not providentially hindered. The English poet and hymn writer, Frances Ridley Havergal, said, "An avoidable absence from church is an infallible evidence of spiritual decay." Take time the evening before, and on the Sunday morning, to prepare your heart to meet with God, through reading, prayer, and praise, individually and as families. Remember that the corporate worship of the church is the pre-eminent means of grace for God's people. Go to church as often as you reasonably and profitably can. Do not get into the habit of gathering with God's people only once when you can do so more often. Do not treat the services of worship as a painful burden. Bear in mind that different churches in different situations may order their Lord's day differently to what you are used to, so do not crassly assume that different is wrong! Make the most of the whole day, giving yourself first to the public worship and then to other opportunities for real spiritual fellowship with God's people, or the private pursuit and enjoyment of communion with God.

Put away (physically, if necessary) those things that are likely to distract or tempt you from a right use of and greatest blessing from the Lord's day. Switch things off, leave them at home. Walk away from things that will hinder you from seeking after God without distraction.

Plan the day in order to get the most benefit from it.

Think how carefully you do or should plan your time on a typical workday in order to accomplish the maximum amount. Think how you prepare for a special occasion. Does God's day deserve anything less?

Do what you can to review the morning worship at or after lunch. Work over the exposition and application of the Word of God either alone or as a family. There might be opportunities at the end of the day to gather as a family or with friends for a similar exercise.

If you are the head of a household, or have sufficient influence or authority, consider conducting family worship in the morning or afternoon. There are likely to be few other days of the week when you have so much opportunity to sit down as a family. The afternoon might also be an appropriate time to review the morning sermon.

Consider appropriate physical exercise. Some people will not be able to use the day wisely without working off Sunday lunch, or at least getting a breath of fresh air. Going for a walk or a bike ride may help to brush off mental and physical cobwebs. This does not mean that going to the gym, or playing a round of golf or a game of football or cricket, or whatever else, are a good use of time on the Lord's day.

Consider appropriate physical rest. Some people will not be able to concentrate on (or even be present at) the evening service unless they take some kind of break during the afternoon. Having a snooze or 'power napping' are not wrong, as long as they are not the product of mere laziness.

Pursue Christian fellowship. This is a day on which some might be able to offer hospitality to others (especially those who might otherwise have nowhere to go) in a way not possible at other times. Perhaps church meals are a good idea, or prayer meetings, or discussion groups meeting after the church, or a chance for people to meet with the preacher and follow up his preaching, or ask other questions. Even simply sitting and then talking with someone who cares, at or around the church services, might be a big deal to a lonely Christian, or to someone unconverted who never normally has Christian company.

What about reading? Many Christians today complain that they do not have time to read the good books that they would like to. This might be a good day to catch up on Scripture reading, or to set aside some time to read some of those books you have always intended to. Consider that if you read for just one hour every Sunday of the year, you will have read for 52 hours each year. Imagine what progress you could make! Perhaps parents could read something with their children.

Practice and develop the art of godly conversation. At first, this may seem difficult, and feel very artificial and falsely 'pious.' It is not necessarily wrong to talk about certain pressing things of this world, and consider them through the lens of revelation. However, this is your particular opportunity to put aside your usual interests, worries and concerns – politics, economics, entertainment, your job and its pressures – and feed your soul on the things of God. At the very least you can take time to put those interests, worries and concerns more firmly into the context of God's word.

There are many works of mercy that are appropriate for the Lord's day. Some of them might be spontaneous--remember the animals falling into the ditch. Others might be more deliberately planned and executed. While we should not be doing those things which could reasonably have been done during the week, we ought not to suspend such works on the Lord's day. Indeed, there may be some who are not able to do these things during the week, for whom the Lord's day would be the ideal opportunity to undertake such ministries of mercy. Are there not widows, the elderly, the sick, or others in need, for whom we could in some way provide, or at least encourage with a visit, during the Lord's day?

This might be a good opportunity for evangelism. You could go out on the streets, invite people directly to the services, or invite friends to be involved in a church or family meal. Remember, though, that we cannot legitimise what is not right on the Lord's day simply by inviting or involving a few friends and neighbours. The best testimony to unconverted men and women is not to involve them in our neglect of the Lord's day, but to show our obedience to the Word of God.

Children, particularly younger children, might find these things difficult, especially at first. Making them take a long nap can be cheating! Think about ways of making the Lord's day a delight for your children. You might buy them 'Sunday best' clothes that they wear only on Sundays. Have a box of activities that are reserved for and appropriate for Sundays. Perhaps just spending time with them – even walking and talking – would be a big step in the right direction? For some kids, that could make Sundays the bright spot of the week, a real expression of what it means to have a godly dad or mum. It might be an opportunity that does not come on any other day of the week.

CONCLUSION

The way to preserve and protect the Lord's day is not to revise it, or to over-regulate it, or to reject it. It is to restore it to its proper, biblical place. Our aim must be to keep it as God intended it to be kept, on the basis he gives us for it, for the purpose for which he intended it, by the guidelines he provides for us.

No doubt this might sound very demanding to some. It is easy (and, up to a point, reasonable) to think, "But if I do this, then (insert disaster of choice) will certainly or possibly happen..." In such a case, we need to remember that there is a cost to discipleship. There is a price to pay for biblical Christianity, and our Lord himself instructs us to count that cost (Luke 14:25-33). We must take up the cross and follow Christ (Matthew 8:34-38). Obedience to God and nonconformity to the world has always been costly, but we are to consider both the reward and the warning: "those who honour me I will honour, and those who despise me shall be lightly esteemed" (1 Samuel 2:30).

> Here is the patience of the saints; here are those who keep the commandments of God and the faith of Jesus. Then I heard a voice from heaven saying to me, 'Write: "Blessed are the dead who die in the Lord from now on."' 'Yes,' says the Spirit, 'that they may rest from their labours, and their works follow them.'"
>
> — REVELATION 14:12-13

So consider the encouragement of Jonathan Edwards:

> those who have a sincere desire to obey God in all things, will keep the Sabbath more carefully and more cheerfully, if they have seen and been convinced that therein they do what is according to the will and command of God, and what is acceptable to him; and will also have a great deal more comfort in the reflection upon their having carefully and painfully kept the Sabbath.[1]

'Painfully keeping the Sabbath' does not mean that embracing the Lord's day brings pain of some kind! It simply means, in this context, something that demands effort and exertion. So yes, there may be a little 'pain' involved. But Edwards is simply saying that whatever the cost, in time or energy or anything else, of keeping the Lord's day, it will comfort us to know that this is pleasing to God. It may not be easy. Keep it in the right spirit and with the right motives, though, and you will find it a true blessing.

You may also be thinking, "All that may be so, but it is beyond me." Let us go back to the beginning. On what basis does God require this of us? It is on the basis of our redemption. We have been freed from the bondage of sin and liberated from the world in order that we might obey God. We have become slaves of righteousness, obeying from the heart that form of doctrine to which we were delivered. Salvation is beyond us, as is obedience, without the resurrection power of the Christ who is the Lord of the Sabbath. Do we feel ourselves weak, useless, and weary? In him is grace, strength, and power. We are to stand, strong in the Lord, and in the power of his might, trusting in him to help us in all the glorious privileges and duties of our lives as children of the living God. We are to keep the resurrection day of Christ in resurrection power. We are to obtain our power, in measure, by communion with the risen Lord on his day.

Ignatius of Antioch (c.35 c.107), an early Christian martyr, urged his fellow believers to "let every friend of Christ keep the Lord's Day as a festival, the resurrection day, the queen and chief of all the days." Do we do this? Could we sing these words from our hearts?

> *Christ is risen! Hallelujah!*
> *Risen our victorious Head!*
> *Sing his praises! Hallelujah!*

Christ is risen from the dead.
Gratefully our hearts adore him
As his light once more appears,
Bowing down in joy before him,
Rising up from grief and tears.

Christ is risen! Hallelujah!
Risen our victorious Head!
Sing his praises! Hallelujah!
Christ is risen from the dead.

Christ is risen! All the sadness
Of his earthly life is o'er;
Through the open gates of gladness
He returns to life once more;
Death and hell before him bending,
He doth rise, the Victor now,
Angels on his steps attending,
Glory round his wounded brow.

Christ is risen! Henceforth never
Death or hell shall us enthral;
We are Christ's, in him for ever
We have triumphed over all;
All the doubting and dejection
Of our trembling hearts have ceased;
Tis the day of resurrection,
Let us rise and keep the feast.

This day—the Lord's day, our chief of days—should be

an ever-increasing delight to our souls. It should bring delight to the souls of the fellow-members of our churches and the fellow-members of the body of Christ. It should be a witness to a world wasting its time on empty pursuits. It should bring glory to God and blessing to Christ's church, ages without end.

NOTES

INTRODUCTION

1. John Sutcliff, "The Authority and Sanctification of the Lord's-Day, Explained and Enforced in a Circular Letter from the Baptist Ministers and Messengers, Assembled at Northampton, June 6, 7 and 8, 1786," (author's scan), 2.

1. THE PRINCIPLE OF THE LORD'S DAY

1. That is, God set it apart to himself, for a special purpose.
2. R. L. Dabney, "The Christian Sabbath: Its Nature, Design and Proper Observance," in *Discussions of Robert Lewis Dabney* (Edinburgh: Banner of Truth, 1982), 1:548. We will look at the Christian's extra reason later. My point here is that we have one reason as created beings.
3. Sutcliff, "The Authority and Sanctification of the Lord's-Day," 4.
4. An omer is an ancient 'dry measure' -- way of measuring dry goods by volume.
5. Accretions are deposits laid down over time which eventually accumulate to make something bigger.
6. Bruce Ray, *Celebrating the Sabbath* (Phillipsburg: P&R, 2000), 65-66.
7. Sutcliff, "The Authority and Sanctification of the Lord's-Day," 3.
8. Sinclair B. Ferguson, *The Sermon on the Mount: Kingdom Life in a Fallen World* (Edinburgh: Banner of Truth, 1987), 71-75. It is worth reading the whole of Chapter 7 to put these elements in context. For a much fuller exposition of these words, I would suggest Dr Martyn Lloyd-Jones' *Studies in the Sermon on the Mount* (London: IVF, 1959, 2 volumes).
9. Jonathan Edwards, *The Works of Jonathan Edwards* (Banner of Truth Trust, 1974), 2:99.

10. James Nichols, *Puritan Sermons* (Wheaton, IL: Richard Owen Roberts, Publishers, 1981), 2:32.
11. According to John's Gospel (18.28; 19.14), Good Friday was the 14th Nisan; in which case the day of Unleavened Bread of that year was the 16th Nisan, a Sunday. The following Feast of Pentecost would correspondingly have fallen on a Sunday. See F. N. Lee, *The Covenantal Sabbath* (London: LDOS, 1969), 30.
12. Justin Martyr, "The First Apology of Justin," in *The Apostolic Fathers with Justin Martyr and Irenaeus*, ed. Alexander Roberts, James Donaldson, and A. Cleveland Coxe, vol. 1, *The Ante-Nicene Fathers* (Buffalo, NY: Christian Literature Company, 1885), 186.
13. Richard Sibbes, *The Complete Works of Richard Sibbes*, ed. Alexander Balloch Grosart, vol. 5 (Edinburgh: Banner of Truth, 1973), 5:328.
14. Sutcliff, "The Authority and Sanctification of the Lord's-Day," 5, emphasis original.
15. Daniel Wilson, *The Divine Authority and Perpetual Obligation of the Lord's Day* (Forgotten Books, 2012; repr. Boston: Crocker & Brewer, 1831), 125.
16. In the Greek language, this is an εκκλησία --t means, in essence, a group of people called out of the world to God, and so we translate it 'congregation' or 'church', transliterated *ecclesia*. This is where we get the word ecclesiology, for example --he study of the church.
17. Greg Nichols, unpublished class notes on *The Doctrine of the Church*.
18. Justin Martyr, "The First Apology of Justin," in *The Apostolic Fathers with Justin Martyr and Irenaeus*, ed. Alexander Roberts, James Donaldson, and A. Cleveland Coxe, vol. 1, *The Ante-Nicene Fathers* (Buffalo, NY: Christian Literature Company, 1885), 186.
19. Sutcliff, "The Authority and Sanctification of the Lord's-Day," 10, emphasis original.
20. Richard Gaffin, *Calvin and the Sabbath: The Controversy of Applying the Fourth Commandment* (Fearn, Ross-shire: Christian Focus, 1998), 154. What follows is an attempt to summarise and simply Gaffin's helpful argument.
21. Gaffin, 155.
22. Gaffin, 155.

23. Gaffin, 157.
24. Robert Paul Martin, *The Christian Sabbath: Its Redemptive-Historical Foundation, Present Obligation, and Practical Observance* (Montville, NJ: Trinity Pulpit Press, 2016), 262-3.
25. Or, 'every.'
26. Some manuscripts do not have the second part of this sentence i.e. from 'and he who does not . . .' to '. . . not observe it'.

2. THE PURPOSE OF THE LORD'S DAY

1. The idea that we can and should govern ourselves.
2. To use the language of *The Shorter Catechism*, "The chief end of man is to glorify God and enjoy him forever."
3. E. J. Young, *The Book of Isaiah* (Michigan: Eerdmans, 1972), 3:427.
4. David Clarkson, *The Works of David Clarkson* (Edinburgh: Banner of Truth, 1988), 3:206.
5. C. H. Spurgeon, *The Salt Cellars: Being a Collection of Proverbs, Together with Homily Notes Thereon* (Bellingham, WA: Logos Bible Software, 2009), 1:300.
6. Consider, for example, Isaiah 6.1-8; 66.1-2, 14.
7. Richard Sibbes, *The Complete Works of Richard Sibbes*, ed. Alexander Balloch Grosart (Edinburgh: Banner of Truth, 1973), 1:75.

3. THE PRACTICE OF THE LORD'S DAY

1. Sutcliff, "The Authority and Sanctification of the Lord's-Day," 7.
2. Bear in mind he might equally conclude that a leisurely cycle through the beauties of creation, rather than a mad dash to work through the city, might be a suitable way to spend some of his discretionary time on the Lord's day.
3. I take into account some of the issues over the very definition of the word, which I am using here in a fairly generic sense.
4. Bearing in mind also that under the Old Covenant the ten commandments were given to a nation operating as such, with its own judicial framework and distinctive theocratic culture,

which again informs the way in which a Sabbath can be observed.

5. Andrew Fuller, *The Complete Works of Andrew Fuller* (Harrisonburg, VA: Sprinkle Publications, 1988), 3:828–829
6. Sutcliff, "The Authority and Sanctification of the Lord's-Day," 5, emphasis original.
7. Sutcliff, "The Authority and Sanctification of the Lord's-Day," 7.
8. David Clarkson, *The Works of David Clarkson* (Edinburgh: Banner of Truth, 1988), 3:203.
9. Sutcliff, "The Authority and Sanctification of the Lord's-Day," 2.
10. C. H. Spurgeon, *Teachings of Nature in the Kingdom of Grace* (Bellingham, WA: Logos Bible Software, 2009), 161–162.
11. David Clarkson, *The Works of David Clarkson* (Edinburgh: Banner of Truth, 1988), 3:206. For more on the profit and primacy of public worship, I recommend the whole sermon by David Clarkson (1622-1686) from which I have quoted, entitled, "Public Worship to be Preferred Before Private."
12. Sutcliff, "The Authority and Sanctification of the Lord's-Day," 11, emphasis original.
13. I am reminded of the story of the Chinese woman who, upon her conversion, determined to be present at the services of worship on the first day of the week. Her husband was antagonistic to her new convictions, and told her bluntly that the door of the house would be shut and locked at nightfall. The wife accepted the husband's condition graciously. She went to the church services, returned home to a locked house, slept – through all the seasons of the year – outside the home, and waited for her husband to unlock the door on a Monday morning. She entered the home, having fulfilled as many of her obligations as she could on the previous day, and without complaining or recrimination, served her husband cheerfully and willingly. After a prolonged period, her faithfulness to God and her loving commitment to her husband won the man over, and he repented with tears. I say this not to establish an enduring model, but to demonstrate how such convictions can be righteously worked out.
14. C. H. Spurgeon, *The Interpreter: Spurgeon's Devotional Bible* (Grand